Cherished Pets

Letters from Heaven and the Heart

Bradley Spellman
The Pet Shop Guy Since 1968

Cover Photo "Prancer" by the author.
"Sun Through Trees and Fog" by Jarrod.
Creative Commons Licensing

Year of the Book
Glen Rock, PA
yotbpress.com

ISBN 13: 9780991271641
ISBN 10: 0-9912716-4-5

Library of Congress Control Number: 2014947196

ACKNOWLEDGEMENTS

Thanks to these organizations and publications for help reaching out to story contributors:

AKC

Animal Health

Animals Magazine

Anne Arundale Community College

ARK

Birdtalk Magazine

Cat Fancy

Cats

Defenders of Animal Rights

Dog World

Essex Community College

Fate

Horse

Horse &Horseman

Horse Fancy

Dr. Michael Fox, HSUS

Beatrice Lydecker

Maryland ESP

Memo

National Enquirer

Parapsychology Review

Perspective

Pet Business

Pet Supplies and Marketing

Psychic Pets

Readers Digest

Reptiles Magazine

SPCA

Today's Animal Health

WRC-Radio Talk

DEDICATION

This book is dedicated to all pet owners who have loved and lost a pet. It is for all of those brave enough to come forward and share stories of their beloved pets. It is for pet owners who want to believe they will be reunited with their best friend in heaven.

Thanks to my retail customers for this past forty years and their pet stories.

To my wife Kathy and daughter Christine, who have commented on my sensitive side when shedding tears about these tragic stories of pet loss.

It is also dedicated to: Harry, Pee Wee, Puff Ball, Rocky, Tuffy, Igor, Lewis, Green Girl, Sunny, Taffy, Cindy, Puffer, and Prancer, who personally touched my heart.

TABLE OF CONTENTS

INTRODUCTION

All pet lovers agree that the emotional ties between a pet and an owner are inseparable. This intense bond dives deep and captures the depth of our hearts.

When a pet, friend, or close relative passes away, one's entire world experiences a tragic loss. The loss of a best friend can be devastating and ultimately irreparable.

Many seek to attain closure after realizing they will never recover what they once knew. The attempt can be disheartening and in some cases unachievable.

I share with you the captivating and emotional accounts reported to me involving grieving owners and their beloved pets.

Do pets have a way of communicating after they have passed to the other side? Let's take a look.

❧

Much like couples depend on one another for strength and support, many individuals turn to pets for the same sense of companionship. Certainly out of the millions of pet owners, there exists extremely close human-animal bonds.

Knowing how strong this relationship can be, the thought-provoking question arises: Do telepathic communications between owners and the beloved pets exist? Dependent on an individual's faith, is there the possibility that pets join their owners in heaven?

A number of people have shared their stories with me to discuss what they believe occurred, and to seek out others who have had similar experiences. They are not alone. There will be skeptics in the general public who strongly believe they have the answers to what these accounts are all about. Whether we are skeptic or believer, though, we should remember these stories only emphasize that there is a need to probe deeper.

I have collected true accounts from all types of people throughout the United States and Canada who were willing to share their personal experience and "contact" in one form or another with their cherished pet.

With each chapter of the book, many astonishing and enlightening tales of beloved pets unfold. I have collected these stories through personal interviews, publications, and the worldwide web. Within these pages you will read both heartbreaking and heartwarming accounts of the bond between owners and their treasured pets.

During the compilation process, I received letters stating that I was delving into the devil's work, while others told me I was the chosen one and included karmic maps and concentric circles sent to my geographic location.

Many of the contributors acknowledge being taunted and scorned by friends and family members due to the sensitive nature and varying opinions of pet spirituality. When attributing the stories within these pages, individuals are named only by location, first name and last initial so they may avoid further ridicule. These stories share a commonality in pet after-life experience and demonstrate lives touched and love shared between humans and their pets.

I am an animal lover, fascinated by the mysteries these stories hold. There are events in life which cannot be explained scientifically, yet we know in our hearts they exist. The religions of the world contain elements that are widely believed, yet cannot always be touched or measured.

Many individuals around the world have experienced this through the loss of a beloved pet. The shared love between owner and pet may even cross the barrier of death to say goodbye.

MY LOVE FOR ANIMALS

Growing up, I spent most summers on the beach in Ocean City, Maryland. My grandfather owned two houses, side by side, one for him and my grandmother, and one for the rest of the family to use.

While at the beach, I would fish with my dad and brother. We would catch flounder, sea bass, and blowfish. Some days I would collect crabs, turtles, sea horses, and starfish. During our fishing trips, we were often accompanied by my grandfather's faithful dog, Mickey. I would dodge aggressive sea birds attempting to protect their nesting sites. In isolated swampy areas, I encountered mosquitoes large enough to choke a horse.

Clamming on flatbed boats in bay areas was an enjoyable activity for me. Clams could be felt on the sandy bottoms of the bay with bare feet. I would reach down, catch them, and toss them into large wooden crates located on our boat. One day, I peered curiously into the crate containing our clam collection and was whacked on the head with a clam the size of a baseball, tossed by a fellow clam digger.

My father, a school teacher, always had me involved with hands-on activities in nature. Our expeditions included various animal observations during outdoor adventures. My dad was friends with Dr. Watson, curator of reptiles at the Baltimore Zoo. We would often have the opportunity to participate in behind-the-scenes tours.

Years later, I began to visit the zoo frequently and became friends with Janet, the penguin lady. Others I met included: Fred the curator of birds, Dr. Watson, Billy the mammal guy, and Carol the elephant man. I gained an extensive education about exotic animals from my many behind-the-scenes visits with the animals and zoo staff.

Fred had such an abundance of Ostrich eggs he scrambled up a meal for ten from only one egg. This is one of my fondest memories from my zoo visits. Most of the animals had names, special personalities, and special needs which made each unique to the zoo keepers.

At age twelve I caught a seventeen-year old albino locust while fishing in one of Baltimore's watersheds. The locust – the first one found in the country – was donated to the Smithsonian Institution in Washington, D.C. I continued my involvement with animals and nature well into my teen years.

In high school, I won the science fair with a project on blind cave fish from Mammoth Cave, Kentucky, also found in Mexico. I then went on to compete in the Johns Hopkins National Science Fair.

I enjoyed embarking on expeditions to collect sea creatures. Cape Henlopen, where the Delaware Bay meets the Atlantic Ocean, was a popular spot for me to explore. I would time my trips to coincide with low tide, ideal for scooping out creatures from sinkholes and tide pools.

Many of these creatures made their way from the Caribbean on seaweed, arriving via ocean currents. Brightly colored damsels, seahorses, snails, and anemones were plentiful finds. Styrofoam coolers were filled with prepared artificial seawater to match the salinity level of the ocean. This aided my attempt to sustain my precious sea creatures for the ride home.

Once on my three-hour journey home, I was stopped by a Maryland State Trooper. He looked in my backseat, peering at my Styrofoam coolers and asked, "Where's the party?" He wanted to check inside each one! Once opened, he found bags of water with my treasures. I informed him I was collecting marine specimens at Cape Henlopen.

"Sorry to have bothered you," he said.

In 1968 I started my official pet career. I worked at two retail pet stores and for a manufacturer owned by the same company. I started out as a part-time employee, later becoming the manager of one of the stores. I remained there for twenty-three years, working and attending college.

I graduated from Essex Community College and attended York College of Pennsylvania in the evenings for several years. At the start of my pet career, I also volunteered at the Carney Animal Hospital in Baltimore, where I quickly learned the process of loss and grief when pet owners were faced with saying goodbye to their furry best friends.

During the late 1970s, my brother and I helped collect 50,000 signatures at the Baltimore Inner Harbor to influence voters in support of a National Aquarium in Baltimore.

From 1972-1976, I appeared on the nationally televised PBS show, *Love Tennis*. In the 1980s, I provided pets for several nationally televised Chevy truck commercials and for a national jewelry chain commercial.

Starting in 1991, I began working for a chain of pet-feed stores, with locations in Maryland, Pennsylvania, and West Virginia. I started as a manager of a pet outlet in York, Pennsylvania. I then opened my own pet business with a new corporation name – York Pet Supply, LLC – from 1992 until the present. I opened a second location in Shrewsbury, Pennsylvania, which existed for five years, but I found it difficult to manage more than one site.

For twelve years I operated a wholesale pond supply in New Freedom, Pennsylvania. I distributed products under the name AquaSpell Products from Maine to Florida. Pet, hardware, and lawn and garden distributors handled the products. I attended many national pet, pond, and wild bird trade shows – not to mention every type of dog, cat, bird, fish, and reptile show.

In college my favorite subjects were Animal Science, Biology, Zoology, and Oceanography. I served as President of the Baltimore Bird Fanciers, was a state representative for the American Federation of Aviculture, a member of the Defenders of Animal Rights and supporter of the York County SPCA. I marketed pet comfort heating cables for reptile cages nationwide. We established a breeder reference guide in five states through A J Buck Veterinary Supply for Dogs and Cats. I also had the pleasure of owning a Wild Bird Centers of America franchise in York.

Throughout the years, I have met many interesting individuals in the pet business. One of my pet store customers, an Italian restaurant owner, inquired if I ever collected large sea snails. I said, "Yes, I do." He explained that in the old country, they made a dish called Bobbaluce, or snails in red sauce. He wanted to surprise visiting relatives with this dish and asked if I would be willing to collect snails for this event.

I had a trick to retrieve sea snails, looking for the little air bubbles trickling to the top of the sand. I arrived back in time with the snails for the chefs to prepare the dish. It was a huge hit and I was invited to stay and enjoy the meal!

This varied career allowed me to develop wonderful relationships with pets and their owners over the past forty years.

Pets

That

Linger

PETS THAT LINGER

The sun and moon are more than evolving objects in space; they are our clocks, set by all primitive societies and even today's most sophisticated societies for understanding the concept of time.

Time provides a convenient means for organizing our lives, a way of celebrating special occasions we want to remember… and a useful measuring tool for analysis in scientific experiments. Scientists have adapted time measurement from the celestial bodies to establish the extremely accurate atomic clocks.

Our lives and routines are divided into all types of time intervals, ranging from seconds to centuries. Our very life and death are time-stamped on our tombstones.

After death, we do not know whether there is any concept of time as we presently understand it. We can only assume, as most religions of the world teach, that existence after death (end of physical life on earth) is a different type of "aliveness" where there is no need for the kind of sun, moon, stars, or time-keeping devices we rely upon.

Caught as we are in the physical laws of time, we often wonder why things happen. All philosophical, religious, and scientific questions fall into this category. "Why would a former pet reappear at a certain time?" From research into the After Death Pet Phenomena field, we do not have all the answers, nor have we even located all the clues as to why things happen when and how they do.

If time is totally unimportant in the spiritual realm (that realm of existence after death), then we need to discover what other factors may explain a pet's after-death contact with its owner.

However, time is still helpful to any scientific researcher as we look at when and how often (in time) sensations have been reported. Some pet owners are very alert to the time a sensation took place, even showing concern for recording the exact hour of the day, possibly using the time of day as "proof" something truly occurred.

F.W. MURPHY

For ten years, F.W. Murphy (an unusually handsome and intelligent grey tiger cat) was an important member of our family. He had many distinctive habits and was very much a creature of routine. He had his own special swinging door which had been built into a cellar window. In fact, his "door" had its own comfortable porch for him to sun himself upon.

The door to the cellar led to the first-floor family room, and was always left ajar for him, as well as doors leading up two more flights to our bedroom on the top level. (The house was a four-level split with an additional cellar level.)

F.W. came and went as he pleased, but since he had been neutered, he was not a nighttime prowler. He always curled up on the foot of my twin bed to spend the night.

With first daylight, he customarily went downstairs and into the garden – a "plumbing shop," I suspect, though he did have a sandbox. In a few minutes he returned, jumped back on the bed, and went back to sleep until it was time for the family to get up.

We lost him to a kidney problem. He was hopelessly and painfully ill. The vet mercifully was able to end his misery, but we were heart-broken.

Every morning for several weeks afterward, I was awakened by him jumping on the bed and turning around several times before curling up.

8

I am not given to flights of fancy, nor did I see him. But the jolt of his landing on the bed awakened me. I was completely awake when I felt him turning around.

Eventually his visits stopped, but I know for a time he was there.

~Adrianni L., Washington

KIRBY'S GHOST

To really appreciate Kirby you had to catch him when he was on the verge of naughtiness, then look deeply into his eyes. Never have I seen such innocence or betrayal of intention. I knew Kirby for about ten years. He was part of the family I married into. Not a lot was known about his background before my wife adopted him. Whether his biological parents were well acquainted or got together for a one-night stand was the stuff people debated around the campfire on chilly evenings.

Kirby was destructive as a young dog. He insisted on inspecting the insides of stuffed furniture, which led me to believe at least one parent was a Cocker Spaniel. We think perhaps his other parent was a Poodle.

The dog was nameless when he was unceremoniously dumped onto my wife. Our son named him Kirby after a dog character in his kindergarten reader.

His life wasn't easy. He suffered an unfortunate run-in with a car which resulted in serious bone and nerve damage. About the time Kirby recovered from that scrape he was diagnosed with cancer of the gum.

After months of out-of-town care which included radiation treatment he was declared healed and returned to us. His appetite for food and mischief were unabated.

Gradually the years took their toll on Kirby. His excitement for evening walks diminished, and he became somewhat incontinent. X-rays revealed spine damage. Our daily routine suddenly included pills for his back and pills for his piddling.

Then one day, Kirby developed a wheezing problem, and it was back to the vet. The growth of a tumor on one lung restricted his wind passage. Grudgingly we consigned Kirby to another world. Little did we know he wasn't ready.

⁓⦅⦆⁓

My wife had become fascinated with a white umbrella Cockatoo, and Casper's arrival had coincided with the departure of one of our children. Like all cockatoos, Casper had a powerful beak and a chewing desire to match. In the fraternity of cockatoo owners and breeders the little darlings are sometimes referred to as "feathered beavers."

The number one target of Casper's aggression had long been a pitiful looking rubber tree that at one time covered a 14'x8' wall. Unfortunately, Casper's cage and the rubber tree were located within several feet of each other in a covered atrium.

Numerous countermeasures to the pruning raids included an inflated rubber snake, Halloween masks, a "chow hound" motion sensor designed to keep unfaithful dieters away from refrigerator doors, and a battery-operated monkey on a swing.

One by one their effectiveness faded.

Finally, my wife discovered the perfect deterrent for Casper. A battery-operated parrot would rattle off several bird calls whenever it was touched or exposed to sudden changes in light intensity.

We named our new ally "Yakkety," and he proved effective at warning us of bird movements – and also the passing of every airliner that moved between the sun and our house. On a sunny day, this was half of all the planes landing at San Francisco International Airport.

Yakkety's scarecrow talent met all expectations. Simply by perching him near the rubber tree we found we could free Casper from his cage without the slightest concern for the rubber tree's welfare. It was virtually impossible to pass within five feet of Yakkety without triggering a raucous eruption.

There was only one failure of our new security system and it occurred the day after Kirby was euthanized and interred in our side yard.

At about 5:30pm on Good Friday, the day after Kirby's burial, my wife was home early from work and we were preparing dinner. Our kitchen is separated from the atrium by a glass wall which allowed us to observe Yakkety at his post and Casper cowering on top his cage.

A sliding glass door was open so we could hear Yakkety's "Casper Alert" if necessary.

At one point I looked into the atrium and was surprised to see Casper cavorting on an exercise stand between his cage and Yakkety's sentry post.

"Oh, oh!" I said to my wife. "Looks like Casper has gotten over his fear of Yakkety. Now we'll have to find a new scarecrow."

We both looked at the podocarpus gracilior tree that served as Yakkety's sentry post. *Yakkety was gone!*

"He probably fell on the ground and is under a plant," she said when we rushed into the atrium, both to retrieve the scarecrow and shoo Casper out of harm's way.

Where was Yakkety? No, he wasn't hidden under a plant. He was nowhere to be found in the atrium. My wife and I walked back into the house questioning the other, "Are you sure you didn't move him?"

I'm not sure which of us saw him first, but there was Yakkety, perched on the dining room table about thirty feet from his post. We racked our brains for logical explanations. Surely Yakkety had fallen and Beau, our other dog, had carried him into the dining room.

But if Beau had carried Yakkety we would have been alerted by Yakkety's calls. And how would Beau maneuver the stuffed bird onto the dining room table?

The front door was locked so someone couldn't have come from the street to move Yakkety. There was simply no logical explanation. We were left to conclude a supernatural force had been at work. A ghost, perhaps? Maybe something connected with the late Kirby.

Within the next twenty-four hours two other mysterious events took place. A pair of gardening shoes that never ever came indoors was found in my wife's closet, neatly side by side. Later she was standing in the atrium and caught a glimpse of a small dark object running down a hallway. The window was opaque so she couldn't make out exactly what it was, but the color, shape and speed looked like Kirby.

She hurried into the house, hoping to intercept the strange object. What she found instead was our cat standing in the empty hallway, back arched, hair on end, making the distinctive cat growl and looking as though she'd seen a ghost.

~Lynn D., California

DUSTY

As winter and the cold weather arrived, my daughter took in a stray cat in her college townhouse. Rules prohibited pets on campus so she brought it home to me and my six-pound Pomadoodle (a cross between a Pomeranian and Toy Poodle).

I had just contracted acute pneumonia, followed by congestive heart failure, which was further complicated by a diseased gall bladder. Dusty, the stray cat, had a severe respiratory infection, ears loaded with mites, and was six pounds underweight. I became very attached and devoted to him when I also learned he had feline leukemia.

Despite my own problems I brought him back to super health. In short order we got rid of the mites, the respiratory infection and raised his weight from six to twelve pounds, which he maintained perfectly until shortly before death.

Whenever I was in pain Dusty would come to me with a look of "How can I help you?" When my dog was sick Dusty would curl up next to him. When one of my sisters had a heart attack, Dusty stayed by her side. And when my other sister had a knee replacement Dusty was there.

Dusty did a lot of unusual things. Though he lived indoors, many other cats, squirrels and birds came to his lookout window on a regular basis. He even saved the life of a baby squirrel who had fallen out of a tree during a vicious rainstorm. Dusty alerted me of this and I was able to dry off the squirrel and give him temporary shelter.

After four years of perfect health and without warning, Dusty weakened. X-rays showed his leukemia had mobilized. He went through the house to his favorite spots for only short visits. Then his legs collapsed.

I carried him to bed and put him on my pillow. His breath was labored and difficult. I stayed with him and told him how much I loved him.

He looked at me lovingly but I could see he was now in pain. I put my hand on his head and massaged him. I knew he was going to die. Then I started to cry.

Me, a 63-year old man cried because my 5-year old cat was leaving me.

Dusty looked up. He put both paws on my wrist, held it like a person and buried his head between them. Even while he was dying Dusty comforted me.

A few moments later he let go with a deep gasp. His head fell back. He cried. He died. I put a light to his eyes. Nothing. A stethoscope to his heart. Nothing.

I cried. And cried.

I pulled a rainbow covered sheet over him and left his head and ears exposed. For a couple hours I let him lie there. It was like he was sleeping. I brought my little dog Nessie over and she kissed him goodbye. I emptied the refrigerator and prepared it for Dusty's preservation for the night.

The next day I drove him a hundred miles away to Angel View Pet Cemetery in South Middleboro, Massachusetts, where my wire-haired Fox Terrier is also buried.

Dusty gave me the strength and purpose to survive my own ordeal. He came to me at the worst possible time, but there was something special – something divine about him.

My daughter feels God put him in my life for a special mission, and

I've since become super healthy.

Of all the things Dusty did I will never forget his comforting me while he was dying. This was a deliberate act on his part and gave me the strength to accept his short existence as one with a special purpose.

When we live on in the hearts of others, we don't die.

Dusty is very much alive. I think of him every day and feel his presence around me always.

~Spero C., Massachusetts

GERMAN SHEPHERD PLUS ONE

A few years ago, as a parapsychologist, I was brought to a house in Tom's River, New Jersey, to see whether the ghost of a dog would still remain in the house when the house was moved a few hundred feet on another part of the property because of the sale of road-front acreage.

In visiting, my wife and I were first invited to share a barbecue lunch. When we arrived the couple had just finished dressing and were ready for the barbecue. They told me how their deceased German Shepherd had apparently playfully rolled his ball down the staircase though there was no reason for the ball to have been handy to do this. Other indications meant the pet must still be around and they were glad of it, and wanted to know from me and my psychic abilities whether the dog would move with them when their house was moved.

After eating, I said I would walk about the grounds of the place. I went off to the right and immediately sensed something was buried there. When I returned to the couple, I mentioned that feeling. They said their dog was buried where I had walked.

With this success, I decided to try walking to the left and when I did, I got a glimpse of a dog. It was very quick but I was able to describe the dog when I rejoined the couple. They excitedly said the dog I described was the pet they had *before* the one they asked about and that this dog was also buried in the yard.

17

I then went upstairs and walked through the rooms, and in one of them, I sensed a presence. I observed an indentation on the bedspread, too wide for a person to have sat down, but long enough for a dog's body. Upon my return downstairs, I asked the husband if, when dressing, he had sat on the spread. He said he had not, that after the bed had been made it was protocol not to disturb its smoothness!

Since then the house was moved, and I am told there is evidence the dog is indeed still with them as I told them he would be.

~Ellen P., New Jersey

BABE

My daughter-in-law had a white Sheltie (Shetland Sheepdog) with orange spots named was Babe. My son also had a Sheltie which was black and white. The black and white dog got killed by a car in Decatur where they lived.

When my son and his wife came here, they brought Babe and for some reason I didn't like her as much as the other dog that had died. Perhaps it was the orange and white color.

One day they visited without Babe. I asked about her and they said she died. There was no reason unless it was a tumor. They were not sure. That was the end of Babe – I thought.

They visited about four times a year. I was in the living room reading around 3pm. when something caught the corner of my eye.

I looked, stood up, and saw Babe from the middle of her back, no head – as she was going through the door into the hall as she had done many times headed toward their bedroom. She had been dead two months or more.

I said, "They're not here. They are at home in Decatur or they may be in Chicago." (Chicago was where her parents lived.).

I did not go into the hall as I did not think I would see Babe there or in the bedroom. I never did see Babe again and that was years ago.

~ Harriet V., Illinois

BIG DOG

I lived in Long Beach at my ex-mother-in-law's home and she had a big dog who would always come into my room at night and sleep on the foot of the bed.

One evening I sat in the den and he kept trying to get up on my lap. I made him get down because he was so big. He put his head on my feet and kept staring at me and crying. I thought he looked terribly sad. The next day he was struck by a car and killed. I think he knew it and was trying to let me know.

The next experience was at a friend's house, whom I had just met. As I got up to leave, I saw a dog standing in her bedroom doorway. He was transparent. I asked her about it and she told me other people had seen him there also. He had been a pet for about twelve years until his death.

Another experience happened at a friend's home in Riverside, California. I saw a cat jumping and playing and really enjoying himself. This cat was also transparent. I described it to my friend, and she told me it was a favorite pet who had died just a few months before.

I do believe animals exist on a spiritual level and that they are very capable of reading our thoughts.

On a Saturday in August my 14-year old pet cat, Oats, was struck down by a passing car in front of our house. When I found him he was still warm and his only injury was to the left side of his head which killed him. We buried him in the backyard under the pines.

The next evening I watched television on the couch near the glass patio doors. As usual I dozed off. While in the semi-sleep state, I heard a cat meow twice – a muffled sound like the cat was outside the doors. I reasoned that it wasn't Oats because he was dead, so I remained on the couch until I woke up sufficiently to get up and go to bed.

When he was alive, Oats would meow outside the doors until I'd wake up and let him in. Our dog wouldn't allow any other cat in the yard and she was outside, so I figured I must be hearing things.

A day or so later I rolled over in bed and stretched my legs prior to getting up. I felt a familiar lump at the foot of the bed where Oats usually slept. I again felt for the lump but it was gone. Usually he'd jump down and head for the kitchen when I'd wake. He knew I'd feed him before going to work.

A day or so later as I was making the bed, an hour or two after rising, I felt a warm spot at the foot of the bed as I straightened the spread – the place Oats usually took his morning nap. I ran my hand over the spot again but it was as cool as the rest of the bed the second time.

About two weeks later, I again dozed off on the couch. Suddenly I felt a tingling sensation along the outside of my left thigh and the pressure of paws as something climbed over and then settled down in the curve of my bent legs. Next I felt little pin pricks like a happy cat kneading the back of my leg and a slight vibration like a cat purring.

I was afraid to wake up completely and open my eyes for fear it would vanish, so in my mind I asked tentatively, "Oats?" I felt him stir and again climb over my leg to the front of me. By then I was aware the television was on, but I concentrated on Oats with my eyes still closed, lying perfectly still.

He sat in front of me and in my mind's eye I saw him. His head was perfect again and his blue eyes were whole. In my thoughts I said, "Oh, you are healing nicely and your blue eyes are as pretty as ever. I've missed you, Oatie."

He looked into my eyes for a long moment then jumped down to the floor. A second later I heard a faint sound like the muffled closing of his cat door. I had sealed up his cat door with tape to keep out the cold drafts this winter.

I believe that was his farewell to me. I have not experienced anything further of him. He was a very unusual intelligent cat, and if cats have souls and reincarnate, I'd like to have him as a pet and companion again.

~Bonnie P., California

LEAKY

My old dog returned to discipline me a few years ago. A starved, frightened Beagle puppy (I thought) so in need of a home and food that every word brought the normal puppy reaction until he found himself named Leaky, which was fine with him.

He kept all other dogs out of the yard and let no one chase his cats. Though I showed him a proper dog bed, his place was on the foot of mine and there he stayed. The beagle absorbed quantities of groceries and apparently was mostly pointer, reaching a weight of sixty pounds, so there was often a difference of opinion about the bed. I soon learned to take what he left me.

Then he started getting on my pillows, so I fixed him his own, on the foot of my bed, of course. His own pillows and cases and blankets. Yes, your majesty.

For fifteen years he ruled supreme, old and heavy and with a demanding bark when he wanted it.

Then a little dog was abandoned in the street and ran wild for weeks. To my astonishment, Leaky brought him in the yard, into the house and made him welcome to everything but his food dish. I braced myself to lose my old friend, realizing he must be telling me something. However, he renewed his youth enough to play with the little dog for some time before he just got too old.

The day came and we made sure he didn't suffer. The little dog took over and all was calm.

Some two years later, I was aware of a presence in the house. No sound, no movement, but something – and the little dog acted strangely. Stealing the cat food and putting the dishes in awkward places – Uhuh! And there he was on my pillows. So, another pillow on my bed, of course. And more food in the dish and more walks and rides.

Leaky always opened the doors by raising on his haunches and turning the knob. The little dog couldn't reach, so he began bringing in the paper, balancing it precisely in the middle.

One day a demanding bark I had thought to never hear again brought me to attention. Leaky! So all demands being met, the presence finally disappeared and we are carrying on as ordered, yes, sir.

~Margaret D., California

GOLIATH

We had to have our Standard Schnauzer put to sleep two months after he was struck by a car (delayed brain damage). Every night, the dog would jump onto my bed, turn around and lay down. After a time, he would jump down, and do the same with my parents. For about three weeks after his death, we noticed that this ritual, or the actions of the deceased animal, continued. It was as if the dog was still with us.

Then one evening, we felt as though a burden was lifted. The whole family had suffered a severe traumatic loss, and it was very sudden that we felt peaceful. Goliath's soul had finally gone to its final rest. The nightly ritual ceased that very evening.

~*Anonymous*, Pennsylvania

BLOSSOM

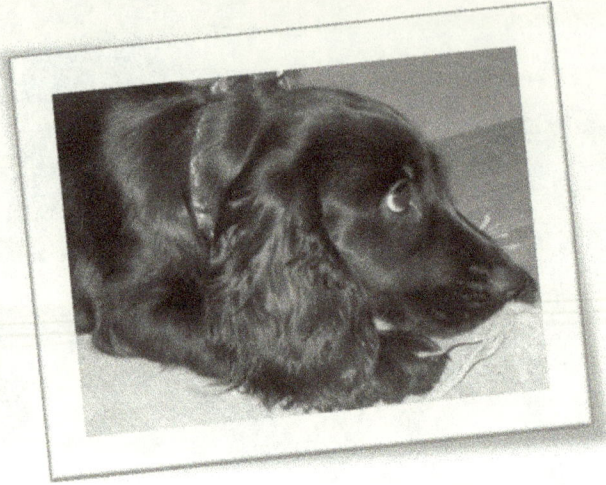

Last November, my beloved dog, Blossom, died – apparently of a broken heart. She had first been the pet of my son and his family, and when they moved to Okinawa for two-and-a-half years, she was left with another son, who subsequently moved to a location where he could not keep her. He brought her to live with me about fifteen months prior to her death. She was as close to human as any animal could possibly be: extremely loving, obedient, intelligent and with a personality that was really delightful. She was five years old when she died.

My son brought his family home for a two-week visit. I asked if he wanted to take her with him when he left, and he said no. He planned to get another dog like her (black mixed Cocker and Labrador). Before they left, he did this and brought the puppy about five days before departure. Blossom went into a depression, which she had never exhibited before. The day they left for Washington State, she came to my son and jumped up, placed her forepaws around his waist, talked to him as though begging to take her with him. He told her no, that she was to stay with me.

Blossom went to his wife and repeated the performance. She also replied no, stay with Mom. Then Blossom ran out to the car and jumped in. They removed her and as they drove off, she watched with her head and tail down.

The next week she never ate, only barked once (though previously she'd been an excellent watch dog). One week after they left, Blossom was moping so much I took her to the vet. At 11am, he couldn't find anything wrong with her. At 7pm, she died.

Twice the following week, Blossom came into my room at night. She used to sleep on the floor by my bed. The first time she spoke her little "woof" (that was her way of saying "hello") as she came into the room and climbed up on the foot of the bed. The second time she merely climbed up without speaking.

I sometimes feel she is nearby, although there has been no further evidence of her presence since that first week. My goodness, how I miss her.

~Anna Jo O., Michigan

GIGI

For eleven years I published *Animal Lovers Magazine*. I wrote occasional articles for the magazines, among them was "Can Animals 'Return' As Ghosts?" I related a personal experience and told of others who had similar experiences. When I wrote the article, I was still questioning the possibility. Today, I am sure that Gigi's ghost was indeed there with us...and still is. (Gigi was a white Toy Poodle.)

Since she died I have recurrently seen white blurs or flashes in our home. I never see it directly but usually out of the corner of my eye or in a situation which makes me turn my head toward whatever was moving. Not only have I seen this repeatedly in our family room, but also many times when typing at my desk.

I thought my white poodle, Taffy, had just walked by my open door, but then I would see her under my desk asleep. So then, what was the white "something" I had seen at that moment and was to see many times thereafter?

I never mentioned this to my husband because he is a non-believer in such phenomena. I didn't want him to think I was crazy. However, imagine my amazement and utter shock when he said a couple of months ago while we were watching TV in the family room, "I keep seeing something white flash by out of the corner of my eye."

My heart started beating fast but I said calmly, "That's Gigi."

"WHAT???" he responded.

And then I told him of the numerous times I had seen the same thing. I asked how many times he had the experience and he answered, "Every once in a while." He hadn't mentioned it because in a million years, he would never have thought it might be Gigi's ghost.

We recently moved to Illinois and I often see something as a blur or movement on the dark carpeting. "My God, our Gigi has come to Illinois with us!" I now accept the fact calmly that she is with us and probably always will be. To establish some kind of definite communication with my little ghost would be my deepest wish.

~Anita C., Illinois

Physical

Objects

Disturbed

PHYSICAL OBJECTS DISTURBED

The loss of a pet can be very traumatic. Many of us have a special connection with our animals, a sacred bond. We know the special sounds our pets make when they jump on the bed and cuddled in against us. We know the feeling of our pet's nails digging into our back or chest. We instantaneously identify our cat's special purr into our ear or our dog's love lick in the face, our best friend's way of rattling the collar and ID tags when it's time for a walk, or the special fluttering of bird wings from room to room.

Your pet has a special scent like no other. You know all of those characteristics. It is the essence of all of these sounds and body movements.

When a pet has passed away and yet the essence lingers – for a day, a week, or a year – only you know those quirky details that made your pet unique from all the other pets you've owned.

Even when your pet has been gone for a month, and you know your friends and family members will think you're crazy, you know what you saw and heard: the sound of your pet playing with a favorite toy under the bed while you try to sleep, the covers on the bed still being messed up in a precise manner, the remnants of unusual treats in usual places even after the pet is no longer with you.

You are not crazy! I've seen my pet's spirit return after the grave. I've heard those special sounds and I've felt them too, even after death. Many of you have had similar experiences, and I thank this book's contributors for coming forward to share their experiences.

HONEY & GYPSY

My constant companion for thirteen years was a female Seal Point Siamese named Honey. I loved her dearly. Honey slept on top of me. She ate when I ate and every time I sat down she sat in my lap. When Honey was nine years old we brought a dog into our home – a small mixed breed that had been deserted. Honey and the dog (which we named Gypsy) became the best of friends.

I always kept a bowl of tootsie rolls on top the dining room table. Gypsy had quite a sweet-tooth. Honey would jump on the table, pick out a piece of candy and throw it down to Gypsy, who would eat about half of it and leave it lying on the floor. This became an everyday affair. Gypsy was short and fat. She'd never been able to jump up any further than the sofa. So, Honey assisted her anytime she wanted something from the table or cabinet.

In February, Honey died, and we buried her in the back yard.

For the first few days I was so upset, I didn't really recall anything happening. But within a week things began to take place.

I thought I saw her a few times out of the corner of my eye. And there were times when I'd hear her crying. I'd wake up at night because I thought I felt her moving around on the bed. Now all those things could have been in my mind.

But two events that took place every day for two weeks were not my imagination.

Every afternoon when I came in from work, I would find a half-eaten tootsie roll on the floor in the dining room – just where I had always found one before Honey died. On further examination, I would find a small green pillow lying in the middle of the living room floor. Nothing so unusual about that except that the pillow sits on the fireplace mantle with a stone cat figurine on top of it. The figurine must weigh about five pounds, and had not been disturbed. It was as if someone picked it up, took the pillow out and set it back down in the same spot. I have several witnesses to both these occurrences. There was no one in the house all day during the time these things took place.

I looked at it as Honey still giving Gypsy her tootsie roll every day. There is no way Gypsy could have gotten one herself.

As for the pillow, I never could make any sense or meaning out of that.

During this period of time, I looked for a Himalayan kitten. I soon found one and brought him home. From the moment I came home with Chan, nothing ever happened again.

I loved Honey so much I really didn't want the phenomena to stop. When it was happening, I could feel her presence. I wasn't scared. In fact, it made her death easier to handle because I still felt a contact, a closeness to her.

~Lynda C., Tennessee

Sensation of a Pet's Death

SENSATION OF A PET'S DEATH

The exact moment of death is an unknown. We know it will happen – to us, to all other humans, and to our pets – but even in the case of terminal illness, the exact day and time of death remain a mystery.

In this chapter, you will hear stories of people who have sensed, or "immediately known" a pet or relative has died.

This "knowing" does not mean the person even realized the pet was sick. Instead, the visited person expresses a feeling of an awareness of the pet's presence – either a physical or mental sensation. Only later does the person learn the pet has died.

How is it possible for a few pet owners to feel those almost exact moments when their pets have passed?

Is it possible that some pets desire so greatly to be with their owners or friends that they are able to visit one last time?

Most accounts in this book are about the usual pets, namely dogs and cats. Are these deceased pets sensed – at the moment of death or thereafter – better than other animals? Are the sensations felt more strongly because they relate to our senses of touch, smell, sight or hearing? Or because of emotional or psychic abilities?

What about other species of animals (fish, birds, raccoons or snakes)? Are they able to reappear after death? What about minute life forms such as bacteria, mosquitoes or worms? Do they have the means to reappear? Philosophically, logic suggests all life forms have equal means to reappear, rather than only dogs, cats, and horses.

Is it possible that a pet can be sensed only by a human being, at that moment, based on the strength of an attachment-bond, while other animals pass on to a spiritual life form without any feelings (emotional or psychic attachments)? This may sound like a very theoretical question, but After Death Pet Phenomena (ADPP) research provides clues and further answers to the importance of attachment-bonds in relation to ADPP experiences.

BUNNIE

I recently lost my dog, Bunnie, whom I had for fifteen and a half years. I am now forty-one years old and when we brought Bunnie into our lives I was in my twenties. She was the first dog I ever owned.

Bunnie was a Pekapoo, and we got her at a pet store in the local mall. It was March 7th near Easter time, and she ran like a rabbit. My two daughters were thrilled. I must say she became a part of me.

Bunnie went everywhere we went. She loved to swim in the pool with us, sleep in our bed, and share our meals at dinner time. Never having the experience of training a puppy, Bunnie trained us.

She wanted to sit near the kitchen table. She used to make sounds with her throat, trying to speak to us. I still remember when we used to go bike riding and she would jump at my bike, so she could go with us. My husband took a plastic milk crate and attached it to the back of my bike and we were off! I still remember how people laughed at the sight, but I did know she was happy to have the wind on her face.

It is hard to describe all the memories of our time together. She grew up with us and sadly grew old. Her last year was extremely hard to watch her slow down, but she was always glad to see us walk in the door.

We knew we had to make a decision in those final months, although it was too painful for my husband to think about. While we were away on vacation this past October, Bunnie became terribly ill and my oldest daughter, Katie, tried very hard to keep her going until we returned home.

Bunnie's last days consisted of all the foods she loved – cheeseburger to steak – bought just for her. The day before we came home she was too ill to even get up. My sister (and dearest friend) went with Katie and Bunnie to see the vet. There was no choice but to put an end to her suffering.

My sister Marion held Bunnie before the injection and kissed the top of her head the way I always did and said, "Tom's here and I love you." Bunnie looked up at that and went to her final sleep. Even the vet commented to my sister that he believed Bunnie knew I was there. While sitting there I felt a pressure on my left lower leg.

At exactly the time Bunnie died, I became quite ill with a severe headache and could not reach anyone at my house. I remember a feeling of dread. I wanted to go home.

My family did not tell me until we reached the driveway of our home. I have never felt such profound sadness. The next day we brought Bunnie home, and buried her in the backyard, under the statue of St. Francis of Assisi.

Exactly one week from her death, I had a dream. During the dream, I was sitting at my kitchen table talking with my sister. I remember saying to her, "There's Bunnie. She came back!" I bent over to kiss her and then I woke up.

I immediately told my husband because I could still feel the pressure on my leg. I was not upset but felt happy to know I got to say goodbye her.

My sister also had a dream about a week or so later. She remembers dreaming she and Bunnie were backstage on the set of the soap opera, *All My Children*. "Bunnie, what are you doing here?" The dog climbed to the top of the rafters, looked down and spoke, "Tell her I love her."

I still feel Bunnie near me. We did eventually get another dog, Angel, because the emptiness in our lives was unbelievable. One night I could not sleep and Angel and I were on the sofa. Even then I could hear

Bunnie walking around in the other room. She will always remain nearby in a corner of my heart.

~Linda M., New York

LUCKY

It was a warm, sunny afternoon and our family walked away from the ASPCA with a very tiny four-week old mixed-breed male dog. It should not have been there or even adopted out because of its age, but whoever took the puppies there claimed they were six-weeks old and eating on their own.

So began the battle of feedings and teaching the puppy to eat. His diet consisted of oatmeal and baby cereal mixed with warm milk so thin it ran off the spoon. After a few unsuccessful attempts, the puppy finally got the idea.

We decided to name him Lucky because according to my mother, "That pup was darn lucky to be part of our family."

As Lucky grew and matured, what started out as a bowtie of white fur under his chin became a white patch across his chest. The rest of him was black, with tan paws and eyebrows.

He was a loyal friend to everyone in the family. If someone had a cold or just didn't feel good, Lucky would be at that person's side. You had to literally pry him from your side until you were feeling better. He had no formal training but listened extremely well.

As the years went by, there were many happy times with Lucky. After a full life and fourteen years, his health started declining. First his hearing, leaving him totally deaf, then his senses. After a nap he'd wake up and go the "potty" wherever he was.

43

We eventually decided the best thing was to put him to sleep. His loss left a very big hole in our family and he is still missed.

About one to two months after Lucky's death, we found muddy dog prints on our upstairs hallway floor. We cleaned with soap and water, stripping agents, and even straight bleach. Each time the floor dried the prints would reappear.

They remained for a couple of months and we also heard toenails clicking on the floor – pacing, checking, going from room to room – as Lucky had done so many times during his life.

We were told that in order to "put his spirit to rest" we must tell him everything was okay and that he should go rest. We did this, and soon the clicking stopped. The paw prints eventually faded and never returned. The physical evidence is gone, but the spiritual feelings are still here. Lucky will be forever in our hearts.

~Cecilia C., Pennsylvania

PEPE & KEMO

A dog that was very dear to me died, and I truly believe that he came and said goodbye to me before he left for whatever becomes of animals when they die. (I hope they have something – I have never met an animal that was bad on his own.)

I have horses and I love trail riding. I always take my dogs with me. (I have two – a German Shepherd and a small mutt.) I am writing about, Pepe, was also a German Shepherd, but not my own (although he spent more time at my place than his own). He always came with us.

When Pepe was two, he took sick. I told his owners I thought he may have heartworm. Unfortunately I was correct.

He was well taken care of but they didn't believe in heartworm at the time. (They do now). His owners took him to the vet for the heartworm treatment.

I didn't see Pepe for some time because he had to keep quiet. I went to visit him, but his presence was missed whenever we went riding.

One day I started out for my regular ride and was out on the trail for about ten minutes, not too far from home. Remo, my Shepherd, dashed ahead like she always does. She turned around and started walking back toward me, stopped about twenty feet away, and looked at something behind me. Then she wagged her tail just a little. I turned around and saw Pepe walking toward us. He was just coming around a bend in the trail.

When he came all the way around the bend he stopped. I was happy to see him, though worried because I knew he should've been indoors and kept quiet. I called him, "Pepe." He came forward a couple of steps, then stopped and looked over his right shoulder, then back at us, like he really wanted to come but could not.

Then he turned and walked away.

I thought, 'Gee. He really must not be feeling himself because he normally dashes all around us.'

I jogged my horse over to the bend. I was going to get him home. He shouldn't be out. "Pepe!" I called again. He didn't come, even though he always came for me.

When I got to the bend, there was no dog. I thought he most likely went home through the woods so his owners would let him in. I finished my ride.

Two days later I went over to his house (no one was around until late at night and I didn't want to bother them) to visit him.

Then Pepe's owner told me he had died. I was blown out of the water. I asked when he died. She said two days prior at the vet's office.

I told her he seemed not the same when I saw him Wednesday. She said she never let him out that day he was too sick.

I went home and cried. Then I remembered when I saw Pepe on the trail, Kemo wagged her tail but made no move to join him. Benji also stood still near my horse. Kemo, whenever she saw Pepe, always ran over to him to play-fight. Not this time.

I know Pepe as well as if he were my own. He came and said goodbye to his trail buddies.

I know he wanted to come with us but something stronger called him – death?

Heaven, I hope. I loved him.

~Susan R., New Hampshire

46

LEO

I believe my pet was alive at the time this experience occurred. I must add that in places I speak as if I knew what was going on in his mind. I am not a trained animal psychologist or observer. The conclusions I have drawn as to the rationale of these pets are the deliberations of my wife and myself.

Leo was a grey and black striped, neutered eight-year-old tom. He was very healthy and extremely friendly toward people. I often thought he might be lured away from us because of his friendliness. He was also a bluffer, howling mercilessly and spitting through the window pane at a passing tom. Once Leo was outside, he did not care to fight and would cover his head and ears, while some aggressive tom was tearing away his fur. It seemed to become my job to protect him from marauding males. This would entail my rushing outside at all hours of the night upon hearing an on-going fight. Sometimes it was not Leo. Most of the time, it was Leo getting pounced upon.

Because of this fear he had, he seldom strayed far from the yard. When he did, he was with his mother. She knew of his difficulty in grasping the facts of life. Occasionally, is she was nearby, his mother, Tugboat Annie, a tortoise shell, toughy and shrew, would intervene for him. Perhaps in an effort to teach him to fight. She weighed 15 pounds and he 26 pounds. She was brassy. She taught him everything he knew. From climbing trees and how to get down again (the most important part) to hiding, to catching a bug. He could not catch mice or shrews...or would not. They seemed to frighten him. He wouldn't touch them. The shrew's squeal always startled him.

As time went on, Annie became frustrated in her efforts to teach him self-reliance. She was battle worn. Females do not intentionally take on a tom, without good cause. Her patience, of which she had little, was worn through. To stress that point, she would hit him a good smack when he cuddled her by brushing against her side.

And she intervened less and less in his "fights." I had to come to his aid more and more. Annie was killed out back on Halloween night, hit by a car from behind as she walked along the shoulder of the road.

She could take care of herself but she couldn't anticipate the careless driving of a human...nor can we.

Leo started to wander farther and farther from the yard, whimpering and looking for his mother. He had lost two friends earlier. One, Topaz, a willful yearling in heat, on the back road. And Ditto, a replica of her calico mother, Copy-Cat, died of an illness. He looked for them for days. He paid even more attention to me then he had before. I was all that separated him from disaster. I was counting the days before he, too, would be killed on the back road.

I awoke suddenly one night, finding myself sitting up, after a 'dream'. The dream was probably an out-of-body experience. I was standing alongside the road a hundred-fifty feet east of our house, on the back road. I saw Leo get hit by a fast moving truck. He let out an ungodly yowl and proceeded to drag himself along the road toward our home. His pelvis had been crushed. He was leaving a trail as he dragged himself. He stopped. He looked toward where I was viewing this terrible scene. As if he saw I was there, he turned and headed toward me, his protector.

I remember thinking, Maybe he can be fixed, as he came closer, whimpering. He was almost to where I was standing (I could not move) when I saw the same green panel truck approach quickly and hit him again, ending his pain. It was then I 'awoke', my heart thrashing against my chest.

Surprisingly, I fell back to sleep as abruptly as I had awakened. When I woke the next morning, Leo was missing. I found him at the side of the road where I had seen him hit for the second time, in my dream. I

48

could see where he had been struck the first time and started to drag himself home. And where he turned and dragged himself to where I found him, there being an awful trail of blood and tissue pieces.

Why did he turn away from home? Did he see me "standing there" at the side of the road? If he wanted to cross the road to safety it was only ten feet from where he was hit. Instead, a trail could be seen heading directly and diagonally across the road to home. Then turning away from home, and diagonally to where I stood-at the edge of the road.

Many animals have been killed along this particular one tenth of a mile stretch of road. It is not any different from any other part of the same road where fewer animals have died. I believe there may be strong earth rays (underground water or lay lines) at that location confusing the creatures to some degree as they enter the radiation.

Or affecting the drivers or both.

~Robert K., Pennsylvania

SOCK

I had the great gift of knowing and owning Sock, a Thoroughbred/Quarter Horse gelding for thirteen years. Whenever something was wrong with Sock, illness or injury, I would have a dream shortly before the accident or illness (usually 1 day before) or when it happened (same day).

The dream was usually the same – I would be walking along a beach (Port Washington, Long Island, where I lived until I was seven years old), and would be searching for my horse's right hind, which had broken off. There were odd discrepancies here – sometimes the leg I searched for was white, while my horse's right hind leg was chestnut.

I would find the leg in the water, washed up on the beach, and wrap it in a towel, and then take the horse and leg to a vet to have it put back on.

The dream always started at the beach and ended in a stall – the same beach and same stall. I would immediately awaken, and go check my horse. On at least five occasions, had I not gone immediately, the horse could have died. Those five occasions were when he had either an injury or illness with a 90% or greater fatality rate.

The dream *never* lied, and I would always find my horse waiting for me at the gate – even in the middle of the night.

One winter it became necessary to put Sock down. He was 25, and had developed a horrible, resistant staph infection of his sheath. He stopped eating, and the "look of eagles" he always had disappeared for the first time. As a pharmacist, and working with a myriad of vets, everything possible had been tried and failed. So I finally decided to let him go. (I did not have the dream this one time.)

After he was dead and buried, I held myself together but gradually guilt became all I knew. I cried every day, all day. Then one night I had a dream which took place on my uncle's farm in Maryland. This was the first place I had kept him.

Sock was running with a band of horses – all of which I had once ridden, all of which I knew were dead. Also, the people there were relatives who had passed away. Nothing and no one seemed to notice me but Sock, who galloped up and spoke, "Why are you crying for me? I am happy and healthy here! I will wait for you here." He galloped back to the horses and off into a mist.

One other time, I was crying and spiraling downward into depression again. When I cried out, "Oh Sock, I've lost you," I felt a reply. The touch of a horse's muzzle on my arm, exactly where he used to love to touch me, was accompanied by a voice I've never heard (except in the previous dream). "No, as long as you hold me in your heart, you will never lose me." Then the feeling was gone.

I know he's watching over me. I still hear him sometimes. When I bought two new horses here in New Mexico, I turned some down because of a "negative" feeling I got when I thought of Sock. It's sort of an odd way to communicate, but it's there and no matter how non-religious I am, or how scientific I try to be, I can't deny it.

~Sandra C., New Mexico

Semi-

Sleep

Experience

SEMI-SLEEP EXPERIENCE

Semi-sleep is that time we crawl into bed and are relaxed but not quite asleep. We might be more receptive to things going on in the world around us. This might be the time we pray, or sort out the issues of the day.

Our mind is still working, but the body may be at rest. Many discuss spiritual happenings for both pets and people during this semi-sleep state. Some have alluded to seeing spirits of deceased relatives and passed pets visiting during these times. Story contributors discuss feeling pets jumping on the bed, after they were no longer among the living. Others discuss hearing all the same sounds such as purrs and barking, exactly the same as when their pet was alive. Many report seeing the spirit of their pet and a deceased relative together.

Are these people having a hallucination? Are these real happenings or are these people in a dream-like state? Could they be wishing something to happen but it is not reality?

I have had the personal experience of seeing the spirit of Jesus Christ, seeing and hearing the spirit of passed relatives and pets. Many of you have your own spiritual beliefs and it will be for you to interpret the messages you receive. Your religious beliefs, or lack thereof, will influence how you decipher these messages from the other-side.

SNOWBALL

A few years ago we had a lovely black cat named Snowball who lived to be eighteen years old and enjoyed good health almost to the very end. She always slept with us in our bed. I awoke one night after her death to feel her walking on top the blankets. This feeling was so intense I could actually see the blankets being pushed down with each step. I knew then she was on another plane and wanted me to know she was no longer suffering and was happy.

~Darline J., Tennessee

PENNY

My son-in-law brought us a Pekingese. It had been given to his father by a man who took it from a former wife out of spite. The man had kicked the dog and didn't want her. She came to live with my husband and me, but we didn't know what to name her. She was a pretty blond, but didn't respond to any names about her coloring. One day she answered to "Penny" so that became her name.

Penny didn't like my husband and wouldn't go to him. We felt it was because a man had mistreated her. It was up to me to make her feel welcome and loved. That wasn't hard to do, for she was so loveable. She got over her shyness with me, but whenever anyone else came around she would hide.

Sometimes I would pick her up and hold her like a baby in my arms and rock her in the rocking chair. She loved that. Over time, she stayed closed to me wherever I was – sometimes sleeping on the bed at my back. She loved me and I loved her.

The vet said she was not a puppy when we got her, but she was with us for several years. Toward the end, she couldn't get on the bed anymore, but slept in a basket next to my side of the bed. I could reach down and pet her. Her health got to the point the vet said it would be cruel to make her endure the pain any longer. Although it broke my heart to think of not having her anymore, I consented for her to go to sleep. I missed her so much.

A couple of years passed and my husband got sick and passed away. I was alone and lonely. It was hard to make any plans. I had heard over the years that decisions should not be made hastily after the loss of a mate.

Alone in the house, my mind was active. I thought of the teachings that I was given and what I had studied myself from the Bible and what I believed – my faith. Bit by bit I began to question it all. It seemed that friends and neighbors thought I was so strong I could get by without much attention. But I was like most other people in the grasp of grieving.

One night I had many questions and doubts on my mind. After listening to the television for the evening I went to bed. Sometime later in the night, I woke and was again troubled. I put the light on and propped my pillow behind my back to think things through once and for all.

After a long period of intense thinking about situations in my life I fell asleep. A voice woke me saying, "Wake up, sleepy head, you've got company."

I looked toward the door and there was my husband with the most joyful smile on his face! I greeted him with absolute surprise and joy. Subconsciously I felt a trembling motion against the mattress at my side, but I was too taken up with what I was seeing.

My husband said, "Look there," as he pointed to the side of the bed.

There was Penny all trembling and wanting to get on the bed!

I reached down and lifted her up to my lap. She kissed me while she trembled with delight. I loved her and talked to her, all the time realizing the unusualness of the situation.

I knew this was a real scene for my benefit alone. I so appreciated it. I knew other people would doubt and think me "funny." I pinched myself hard. It hurt.

I looked around the room, especially at the dust on my dresser. It was real!

My husband walked a few steps and sat on the clothes hamper. We talked for some time. He didn't give me advice as to what I should do or think, but I got the feeling he agreed with me.

After a while he said, "Well, we need to go and let this lady get a good night's sleep. Come on, Penny."

At that, Penny jumped off the bed. He reached down and put his hand under her and lifted her up to his waist. They went out the doorway into the living room. I sat a moment, then got up and went into the living room and turned on the lights. The room was empty.

I have been tempted to doubt my faith many times since, but just for a moment, because then – I remember!

~Etta H., Arizona

SNOWBALL II

I am an animal lover and always had pets. I strongly believe that animals do have spirits which live on after death.

My little dog, Snowball was a white Pekingese. He came to me as a stray. I was unable to find his rightful owner so I decided to keep him. Unfortunately, I only had him for two and a half years but in this short time I became very attached to him.

About a year and a half after I got Snowball he developed a bad heart condition and had to be on medication daily. He lived about one year after this.

I believe in communication after death and I do communicate with my grandmother and other close relatives. When Snowball was very sick, I feared I might have to have him put to sleep. I had prayers said for him that he would die peacefully in his own home. Also I communicated with my grandmother and she said Snowball would die peacefully at home.

Snowball developed dropsy along with his heart condition and the vet wanted to tap him. I was against this and once again I contacted my grandmother for help. She told me this wouldn't help for Snowball would die in two weeks at home.

My grandmother was right. Snowball died within two weeks peacefully at home. As he was dying, I placed my hand on him to give him help on his way over.

My loss was great and the house was empty. When Snowball was living, his favorite place to lie was in front room windowsill. About a week after Snowball's death, I came home from shopping and got out of the car. I looked up at the windowsill and saw a faint image of Snowball sleeping peacefully in the window.

A month after Snowball's death I retired to bed. Snowball always used to sleep with me when he was living. That night as I started to go to sleep I felt something near me. I turned over and saw Snowball close by. I was delighted and reached out to pet him. As I did he disappeared. Several times when I was in the house alone I heard Snowball bark softly.

A couple of months after Snowball's death I went to a medium. It was a group session and when the medium got to me she told me she saw a little white dog beside me. Of course, this was Snowball.

I have not felt or noticed Snowball around for a while now. Perhaps emptiness has been filled, for I have two other dogs – Dolly and Patty Cake. My oldest dog, Dolly, used to show some reaction to Snowball, but his visits are few and far between now. I guess he is content now knowing I have new companions.

~ Dorothy D., Missouri

EEAOO

This "animal ghost" story involves a cat I used to have. She was a black and white short-hair named Eeaoo that my husband and I got as a kitten. When she was three years old she got sick and was left with the vet on a Sunday. The vet suspected feline leukemia or feline infectious peritinitis and thought she would die.

My husband called every afternoon to check on her but she only got worse despite treatment.

She had a habit, each morning when the alarm clock went off, of climbing on the bed and greeting us. She walked around the edge of the bed in a circle.

On Thursday of that week, just as the alarm clock went off, we both felt her walking around the edge of the bed, and we both feared she was dead and trying to say goodbye to us. Later that same day we learned she had died that morning.

~Susan M., Massachusetts

Daytime

Experience

DAYTIME EXPERIENCE

I'm not sure whether a nighttime appearance of a pet spirit is more frightening to some than a daytime experience. I've had both but the night ones were more visual. The contrast is striking with a darker background. These spirit visits were never scary experiences for me, but rather natural ones.

My dog Prancer, a German Shepherd, passed away two years ago. He was cremated and most of his ashes are spread around his favorite places on the property.

Two days after his passing, I headed to work at the store. A floating brown eyeball met me face to face at the top of my driveway. Prancer had big brown eyes, but so did my Dad. I'm not sure what to say.

My wife and I still hear Prancer bark in the house, day and night. We also hear him circling around on the bed during the day.

This chapter's contributors experienced both aural and visual visitations. Each was heartbroken at losing a best friend. Are those pets coming back to say goodbye before moving on to heaven?

LAIRD

My mother and I had a beautiful collie, Laird, who was extraordinarily devoted to us. One morning he had been outdoors. She called for him to come back in, but he wasn't in sight.

I started to walk to work and was about a block away when I heard his feet running behind me. I turned and called his name, but was astonished when I saw nothing there.

I remembered then I had heard his feet, but not the jingle of his collar. It must have been my imagination.

When I arrived at work, my mother called to say she had found Laird's body in the back yard. I still think he was following me.

~Margaret G., Louisiana

KAT

Sometime ago I read your request for psychic information regarding animals. To make you acquainted with Miss Bradley and me, we have shared a home together for thirty-seven years and are both cat people. I think we've never had less than six and sometimes as many as thirty – all rescued animals. Of course, all are altered to prevent more of the tragedy of the "unwanted."

Now, Miss Bradley – we call her "Brad" – is an "old soul". She is very gifted in psychic matters and innately knows about such phenomena. As for me, I attended my first séance at the age of sixteen. I am now seventy-eight. I have read much along metaphysical lines and firmly believe in life after death not only for people, but also for our animal friends.

When one of our cats becomes terminally ill, we always try to keep it in our home, giving it all the love and care and comfort possible. When the cat is ready to "ascend the golden stairs" we put him gently to sleep – so he really never knows when he leaves Miss Brad's arms.

A lovely female feline came to us from a gentleman who was unable to keep her. He had simply called her Kat. She lived with us for approximately ten years. Kat loved Brad devotedly and always spent a short time, sitting on her lap each morning. Time came for her to "ascend the golden stairs." She went out easily, but left two heavy hearts in our household.

Three days later, Miss Brad bounced out to the kitchen and said, "Guess what! Kat came back and sat on my lap this morning. And she's just fine."

Miss Brad often sees or feels the presence of a cat or dog that we have lost. Unfortunately, I do not have that blessing. Brad says no matter what disease or accident took them from us – they always appear whole and happy during those visits.

~ Jean & Brad C., California

DUSHUS

When I was ten years old, I received a beautiful six-month old female Scotch Collie. I called her Dushus. She looked just like Lassie. I loved that dog dearly. She would follow me to school, accompany me on my paper route, and sleep at the foot of my bed. Dushus would never hurt anyone. She was gentle and a true friend.

When Dushus was three years old, she was hit by a car and had a serious leg operation which left her with a limp. That was better than losing her. When she was fourteen years old, she slept outside in the front yard and a German Shepherd ran and jumped on her. He tore her bad leg out of joint.

This hurt me so much. I had seen the German Shepherd's attack from my window because I was walking by when it happened. It was a terrible shock. I watched her face. I will never forget it. I knew I would never see her again. I was sick with the flu at the time and couldn't go with her to the vet.

The vet tried several times to put the leg back into place but couldn't. Dushus had to be put to sleep.

A couple of weeks after she died, I saw a shadow walking in front of me on the stairs. It was Dushus. The figure wasn't solid but sort of hazy. She used to stay downstairs because she couldn't walk up the stairs because of her age.

Seeing Dushus walk in front of me like that was her way of telling me she was all right and not to worry. I didn't worry after that because I knew she would always be with me. I believe when we die we will be joined by our loved ones, including our pets, for eternity.

~ Esther P., Canada

SMOKEY

We are a family of five, my husband and myself and our three children. For six-and-a-half years we were the happy owners of Smokey, a blond Cockapoo (half Cocker & half Poodle).

In August one year, Smokey was out in the woods with my husband and son, who were cutting down trees. One tree accidently fell on Smokey and killed him instantly. We were heartbroken as he held a very special place in our lives. We all "felt" Smokey's presence around us in the following days. He seemed to be still with us. He had died on a Wednesday.

The following Saturday, my son went to work early at the local McDonalds. He did maintenance work and went in early before opening. He was alone in the outer part of the restaurant doing some cleaning. He felt compelled to turn and look behind him, and there beside a booth was Smokey.

Smokey just sat there and looked at my son, and then he was gone. It was as if Smokey needed to say "goodbye" to at least one of us before he could go on to whatever realm dogs go into. After that, we no longer felt Smokey's presence around our home. However, for a few more months, we all continued to have dreams about Smokey.

~Marilyn S., Minnesota

PINCHED NOSE

I had no children and my dog was very important to me and well-loved. My husband loved him, too, but this was *my* dog from just a few days old until the day he died at age fifteen.

Every animal has a certain little way of showing affection. My dog's way, with perfect aim and no pain to me, was to gently run his teeth over my nose.

Sometime after he died, I was taking a nap after work. Not totally asleep, and not with him on my mind, I felt the same pinched-nose feeling. I had to wiggle my nose to separate the nostrils.

My nose was not touching my pillow or the bed. My husband was not there. There was no other explanation. I wasn't trying to conjure a "happening." It was identical to the feeling when my dog would do it.

Of course there was no moisture on the outside of my nose, but it was a very firm, positive nose pinch.

~Mrs. W. C., California

CRITTER

I am sure dogs can sometimes see what we don't. Our Lab-mix Critter had an unusual experience.

When we moved to Cleveland from Chicago, we had a lovely real estate agent named Kattryn. Her husband had been dead only a little while. Kattryn and I talked of life after death and shared books. We even visited a medium together. As the years passed, Kattryn became depressed.

My dog Critter was trained to sleep beside my bed, but never on it as he was a large dog. One night about two in the morning, I awakened to find Critter jumping on the bed.

I pushed him off, but he jumped right back up and resisted when I pushed him down again. He seemed terribly upset about something, but I couldn't sense what it was. Finally, when I was becoming angry, he suddenly relaxed and settled down beside my bed again.

The next morning we learned Kattryn had died of an overdose of sleeping pills. I have to believe she visited me, but I couldn't see her. Only Critter did!

~Jean H., Ohio

Nighttime

Experience

NIGHTTIME EXPERIENCE

Messages from dreams can speak the truth about the real world.

Nighttime is that time between sunset and sunrise when energy and spirits are easier to see. Nighttime is more magical, more spiritual, creepier and more ghostly.

Have you ever taken a shortcut through a church cemetery at night and tripped over an old oak tree root?   I fell in the middle of the cemetery with my heart racing. I can't say I saw any ghosts but I wasn't comfortable lying on the ground with the dead either.

Many pet owners have an after-death pet experience at night. I believe the reason this is so common is that many of us allowed our pets to sleep with us and have shared special bedtime bonds.

Nothing prepares us for the loss of a pet or loved one. Unexplainable things happen in this world all the time, but we know some are more than mere coincidence. I enjoy investigating the unexplained happenings to seek answers to the truth about living and dying.

One night I dreamed about our store's pet python. It had broken out of his cage and was going to eat all the pet guinea pigs in the small-animal room. I sat up in bed. The dream was so vivid at two o'clock in the morning.

I drove to the pet store to investigate. The ten-foot python had in fact broken out of his cage. The small-animal room door had been left open, and the python was lying next to the guinea pigs. Somehow I was sent a message from the guinea pigs to save them from being eaten.

TAFFY

Taffy had been in the veterinary hospital since the previous Thursday night. She had been operated on for tumor of the pancreas on Saturday and was a very sick little girl. Between 5:00-6:00 am, my husband and I were awake, trying to return back to sleep. Suddenly, I heard Taffy's foot pads in the other room, walking. I asked Tom if he heard her too, and he replied, "Yes."

Suddenly, she was on my side of the bed and I was talking to her. I think I saw her but I can't be absolutely sure. All I was positive of was talking to her. Tom heard her, but didn't see her. We thought she had died, but when we called the hospital in the morning they sent her home to us.

On March 13th, Taffy was put to sleep in my arms. Her tumor had come back and she had suffered so much for over a year, we decided to put her out of her agony.

I took two aspirins at bedtime so I would sleep. Three hours later, I took another aspirin. I was sleepless. With closed eyes, I knew she was trying to come through to me. First I saw her two eyes and then her dear face, trying so desperately to visit. She vaguely made it and then went. I finally fell asleep.

In my dream, I got out of bed, went into the kitchen, and suddenly she was there with me. She was strong and well. I said, "Oh, Taffy, you're alive. I love you, Taffy." She laid down on the floor and I sat beside her, smothering my face in her beautiful golden hair.

She was solid. I fed her some meat and she ate it. I looked at the clock before and after. She was with me thirty-five minutes.

One of our children came into the room, and was surprised to see Taffy, knowing she had just been put to sleep. I didn't mention anything about my seeing the dog. I wanted to see if the child would notice her. She did and said, "Taffy, it's you. You're alive." We both played with Taffy for a while until she went to the kitchen wall and through it, disappearing.

On April 11th, I prayed Taffy would come to me. I dreamt or saw her jump on the foot of my bed while I lay there. She had two long sticks, sticking on her right side. It seemed as if she had come through woods to get to me. It looked like she had a hole in her right side where pus and blood had dried. I pulled off the two sticks while talking to her and broke them in two pieces. There was a small one on the other side that I removed, too. One of the sticks was wrapped under her fur, and when I went to pull it from her, she started to bite me, but so gently the teeth didn't sink through my skin.

I loved Taffy, talking to her and patting her hair. Finally she stood on the bed and tried to put the sticks in her mouth. I placed them in her jaws but tried to hold back on the small stick that I was sort of sitting on. She shoved her paw under my rump and tried to pull the stick out.

I figured if I was able to keep the small stick, it would be proof that she had come to visit. I put the small stick in her mouth then she jumped from the bed, went to the wall, carrying the sticks and disappeared through the wall.

Her last and final visit was April 24th. In a dream, my daughter and I were in the kitchen. I felt I had to go into the living room. Taffy was lying on the rug there.

"Oh, Taffy, you've come back to see us again." I got down on the floor to love her. She jumped up and started slobbering kisses all over my face. She nearly knocked me down with her excitement and affection. She was happy to see me. As happy and excited as I was. I called my daughter, "Come here quick. You'll never believe this. You have to see it."

When she came into the living room, Taffy looked at her and ran from the room. She quickly returned, jumping on her, slobbering kisses on her face. She was with us about ten or fifteen minutes before going into the bathroom and disappearing into the wall under the sink.

I have never seen her again, but I know she is alive in the other world and is waiting for me, and has forgiven me for putting her to sleep.

~Dorothy T., Massachusetts

CANARY

About cats and dogs I cannot tell but I had a pet canary that I loved. One fine spring day I hung its cage on the front porch so it could get some sun for a couple of hours. However, I was unthinking in that there was a draft and the canary became sick. I did what the pet shop recommended but there was no improvement. When I would run water a song would be literally torn from its sick body. One night about two months later as I covered its cage I gave it a mind message that told it I loved it dearly but that I also knew it would be better off if it could no longer function as God intended. The following morning the canary was dead.

A few nights later I was almost asleep, with my left ear on the pillow. I heard a canary in full song. I lifted my head and it stopped. I laid my head back and it continued.

I then came to the conclusion my neighbor had bought a canary. Not so! The next night the same thing happened. When I turned my right ear to the pillow, I did not hear it!? After four or five days, it finally hit me that it was my canary telling me it was again well and happy.

After I recognized the fact, I never heard it again.

~Faye W., Virginia

SCHNAUZER

My husband and I were very fond of our female Schnauzer, who went with us everywhere and was allowed to sleep between us at night. Shortly after she died of diabetes, I felt her jump on the bed. I could actually feel her walk up to her place in our bed. This happened twice. The second time I mentally spoke to her, saying it was time for her to be on her way and how much we loved her. She never "visited" again.

Perhaps her "visits" gave us an opportunity to say goodbye since that did not happen at the time she was "put asleep."

~*Anonymous*, Connecticut

ZAK

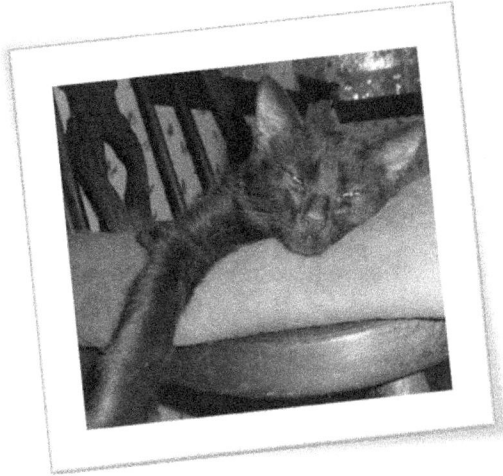

We had a black and white cat named Puff that a neighbor gave to our youngest daughter.

Three years later, a very thin, ill black cat came to our house in the spring. Of course, my four daughters and one son fed the poor starving beast and named him Zak. My husband who was not a cat lover, objected, but was overruled.

I found out why Zak's owners left him. He sprayed the porch and hedges very liberally. My smallest daughter really loved Zak. We all loved him with the exception of my husband. I took the cat and had him neutered over the protests of my husband. I just couldn't bear to take him to the SPCA when he could have a good home with us.

He was such a loving cat, and his continuous meowing delighted the children. He would meow even when he was stretched out on a chair and someone would walk by him. Our youngest (at age twelve) claimed ownership. Zak loved attention and he was the gentlest, most loving animal I've ever had the pleasure of being with.

Our granddaughter was born in April four years later, and came to live with us. The day before we brought her home, I scrubbed the bassinette and got everything ready for the next night.

I found Puff curled up and asleep on one of the family beds, where he sleeps all the time. I spent a half-hour looking for Zak, calling him and going outside. I searched the house and finally, when I walked past the bassinet, I heard his familiar meow. Zak was curled up underneath the skirt of the baby's bed. He always slept underneath her bed thereafter, which led me to believe that Zak had previously been in a household with a baby.

Our granddaughter became attached to Zak, and Zak also loved her. I fell into the habit of putting her in bed with me and singing her to sleep before putting her in her crib at night. Zak always came into my bedroom and would sleep under the bed. When I would start to sing, he would come from underneath the bed and sit at the door.

There were two doors in our bedroom, sliding white doors that the light shone through. As soon as I would get out of bed to let him out of the bedroom, he would run beneath the bed, and go to the other door to be let out, and run upstairs. I never could figure out why he did this.

Zak became sick two years later in February. After three days he died on the way to the vet. My daughters were with me, and Zak struggled in the car trying to escape. He was always afraid of cars. He actually got sick at his stomach when we took him to be neutered. I always believed, and still do, that the poor animal remembered his experience of being abandoned, and he probably thought we were going to abandon him also.

Needless to say, we all missed Zak and I've always believed his death was caused by the way he struggled in the car on the way to the vet, although the vet says not. His bladder ruptured from uremic poisoning.

Anyway, I had the poor cat on my mind for a long time. Two weeks after he died, I was singing my granddaughter to sleep in our bedroom when she suddenly sat up and looked at the doorway. I also sat up just in time to see Zak's long black tail disappear underneath the door.

I got up, turned the light on, and looked underneath the bed, and all over the bedroom, too. No cat! I did what I always did when Zak was in the room. I opened the other door. I believe he left the bedroom in spirit form and went upstairs as he usually did, although I didn't see him, but rather felt him.

My granddaughter looked at me and said, "That Zak, mum?" I also checked with my daughters. One had let Puff outside so it certainly wasn't him under my bed.

A few days later, I was sleeping very soundly. It was Zak's habit to stand outside our bedroom door and meow until I got up to let him out. I heard the familiar meowing that early morning and awoke instantly. It stopped when I sat up in bed.

I've not had any more experiences with Zak's spirit since then, but I do believe he somehow let me know he was happy and content in another life.

~Jean V., Pennsylvania

KATY

A little kitten came to me and I didn't feel as if I would have her very long. Katy was soon run over on the highway in front of my house. Her body was so flattened my parents could not bury her.

Katy's favorite toy was a bell that she rolled about under my bed at all hours of the night and day.

The night following her death, I was awakened by this sound. We had no other animals at the time, and there were no drafts in the room. After about a week of hearing the bell, my mother mentioned to me that she had been hearing it as well.

Mom theorized Katy did not know she was dead for a while.

~Sharon R., Oklahoma

MISSY

My first experience was while I was a teenager. I had an usually strong relationship with a pet cat my mother had taken in as a pregnant, starving, abused stray. Missy became my constant companion. She insisted on my presence when she had her kittens, followed me on long walks at the beach, and always slept on the bed next to my pillow – many times with her head resting in my upturned hand. She even ran out in front of me one day and fought a Weimeraner she thought was attacking me. He was really only running up to say hello but all dogs were enemies to Missy.

She was a great hunter and killer of birds, having had to hunt to live before we took her in. Yet, she never tried to harm my pet Cockatiel which was allowed the freedom of the house.

Missy never tried to harm any other animal I brought home as a pet, although she did occasionally display jealousy with a pet duck I rescued until it was well enough to be let loose at a local game preserve. Missy happily herded it back to the canal where I'd found it!

Because of her bird-killing tendencies, which distressed me but which I understood to be natural, I kept a bell collar on her with her name tag and an additional cowbell attached. She eventually learned to stalk without ringing the cowbell and subsequently still caught birds. I left the bells on, however, because they allow me to know when she was about.

The details are still painful for me to think about, but Missy died when my parents had her put down just before I left for college. She was only five or six years old and healthy at the time. My parents also had Missy's daughter Charlie put down at the same time when we left for a two-week family vacation.

When we returned home, the house seemed unusually empty. Every night for weeks I heard the bells jingle through the hall, come into my bedroom, jump up on the bed and then be still. I would waken in the middle of the night, sure that I felt the weight of Missy's head in my hand or the touch of a small cold nose or soft warm fur.

I thought I was crazy until my sister haltingly asked one night if I heard anything in the hallway during the past few weeks. After some questioning it all came out; she'd been hearing Missy's cowbell, too.

Whenever I was home from college, I would hear the cowbell come into my bedroom at night. My little cat stayed with me until I moved out of state. I haven't heard the bells since, but often think of that wonderful little companion who was always so loyal.

~Stephanie L., Georgia

CURTIS

We had a very sweet Boxer-Bull mixed-breed dog named Curtis. He was dying agonizingly slowly of multiple internal and brain tumors which the vet thought to be malignant. Curtis would cry so much of the time; it was heartrending.

He could not see and would walk stiffly into a corner of the yard or a prickly holly bush and not know where he was or how to get himself out of his entrapment. Curtis had to have help to lie down and then help much of the time to get up. He wasn't comfortable any way he positioned himself. The vet suggested we put him "to sleep".

Since I was the one who spent time with him, I was so aware of his pain. I wanted to do it but my ex-husband (who was seldom home and always gone on weekends and slept through Curtis' nighttime episodes) was reluctant to do so. Finally, however, he agreed to end the suffering. The ordeal was very difficult for both of us and we grieved Curtis deeply.

The problem was that his death did not really seem to solve the problem. Curtis could still be heard several times a day and usually in early evening – crying out in pain.

I related these occurrences to my ex-husband and he didn't believe me. I don't know what motive I had to falsify, but he was totally unbelieving. This continued from late October until early the following

April at which time my husband finally heard him crying under the house directly under our bedroom.

He heard Curtis knock against some boards which were stored there. This sound was a common one when Curtis was alive because he used that section underneath the master bedroom for his dog house. It was raised about four feet higher than the rest of the lower floor to form a split-level.

My husband was awakened and went running out back, pulling on his robe as he went. He took a flashlight and I heard him call to Curtis. He did not see the dog, but finally believed it was Curtis trying to communicate.

This last attempt to get his master to hear him and acknowledge him was rewarded. I never from heard Curtis again.

~Novelle F., California

Sense

of

Sound

SENSE OF SOUND

The sense of sound is auditory perception and vibrations carried to the ear. Perceived sounds received by our ears are more commonly known as our hearing.

When it comes to our pets certain sounds may have special meaning. We hear dogs barking, growling and howling. The rattle of the collar and id tag may have a special sound. The circling around the bed and nails clicking on the floor make distinctive sounds. The clanking of food bowls and the swat of a tail on the storm door are recognizable by any pet owner.

Cats purr, meow, and make soft paw thuds when leaping from one elevation to another. Distinctive litter pan scratching sounds, the excitement of chasing a fly, or climbing the walls after receiving a new dose of catnip or pouncing on a wild mouse are perceptible and distinguishable to pet owners.

Parakeets, canaries, and parrots all have different sounds. Parakeets make a distinctive chirping sound and canaries have a soothing song. Parrots imitate human speech, and scream, squawk and whistle. All pets make distinctive sounds that may have special meaning to pet owners. This is the special language and communication that exists between you and your pet.

OUT TO PASTURE

I really thought my daughter and I were the only ones to believe our animals come back to see us. We often heard our deceased horse at the time of day she always had her last meal.

My daughter took a picture of the horse's grave where we buried her in our pasture. On the picture we see a small imprint of a horse.

I swear to you I think our dogs also feel the horse's presence in the pasture. They stop and look at the tree where she always stood.

When we buried her, we put the ashes of our Doberman in the grave with her. We said it was so they could still run and play together. As we were doing that we heard her whinny.

We are believers.

~Lea B. and Judith H., Maryland

FLUFFY

We had a collie who died in November. She was a family dog, and was very protective of us. On weekends when we didn't get up at our usual time, it was Fluffy's habit to come upstairs and walk down the hall, pausing outside each bedroom to listen. If she did not hear anyone, she would go back and lay at the top of the stairs to wait.

Fluffy died on a Tuesday evening. The following Saturday both my mother and I heard her in the hallway. In fact, it woke me. Even after I was wide awake and sitting up, I could still hear the jingle of the license tags on her collar heading back toward the top of the stairs.

By the next weekend we had a successor in the form of a one-and-a-half year old Keeshond and there was no repetition of Fluffy's visit until the incident below.

Several years later my parents moved to Florida. Not long after, I was at our summer place in the Pocono Mountains (where Fluffy was buried) when I heard her again.

I heard a single sharp bark not more than twenty feet away from me, and again the jingle of her collar. I looked up but couldn't see anything. It was the bark Fluffy used when she wanted to draw our attention to her needs.

There were no dogs on the neighboring properties. Before I mentioned my experience, my sister told me she heard Fluffy earlier that week at her house. She owned a house right next door. After hearing a single bark, she went outside but couldn't see a dog.

Her own dog went out with her. Brandy did not bark as she would have if she had seen another dog, but her hackles were up and she stared at an apparently empty spot on the lawn.

My sister recognized the bark as Fluffy's. Other than Brandy, there was no dog in sight. Both incidences occurred about two weeks after my parents left for Florida.

When we were growing up, Fluffy kept close tabs on all family members including my cousins who spent most weekends at the summer place with us. We felt she was distressed when members of her family were "missing."

It sounds silly but I spoke out loud to her and explained that Mom and Dad were okay and would be there the following summer. We have not heard Fluffy since then.

It's comforting to know she's still watching over us even if we can't see her. We still have the summer place where we can be close to her.

~S.K.H., Pennsylvania

MITTY

Some friends have thought I was dreaming when I had the following experience, but I know I wasn't.

Two years ago our fifteen-year-old half-Siamese black cat stopped eating. We took her to the vet, and after examination he recommended exploratory surgery. We thought about it over the weekend, then decided to go ahead.

After an unhappy experience having another cat "put to sleep" I prayed that when our beloved Mitty died, she would die peacefully in her sleep.

After a suspense-filled morning, we finally heard from the vet. Mitty died after surgery, before coming out of the anesthetic. She had been filled with cancer, and if she had survived surgery she wouldn't have lived much longer. She would have suffered more pain.

After recovering somewhat from our sense of loss, we were able to see her passing was for the best. In a way, it was an answer to my prayers.

Mitty was a house cat. We kept her in at night, and it had been her custom to come to the top of the stairs and call to us. She had the Siamese voice, and the Siamese penchant for "talking" around four o'clock in the morning. I would get up, pet her, feed her, and let her out. Whatever she wanted.

The morning after she died, I was sleeping soundly. I was dreaming, though I've forgotten what the dream was about. Around four o'clock, Mitty called to me from the top of the steps.

I know she came back to tell us goodbye. I said goodbye to her and told her I loved her, without getting out of bed. She's never been back.

~Tracy K., Florida

DAX

Friends of mine used to own a large Boxer whom they kept in their basement or on the landing by the grade door. He grew old and grey and finally died.

Several weeks later I visited. My friend and I sat watching television and talking after her husband had gone to bed. All of a sudden I distinctly heard the sound Dax had always made while asleep — guttural noises half between moaning and growling but contented and sleepy sounding like he was dreaming!

I turned to my friend and asked, "Did you hear that?" She smiled and answered that she had been hearing those same sounds ever since the dog died. She had wondered if it were her imagination.

I called several weeks later to ask if she still heard Dax, and she told me the sounds had finally stopped.

I know it wasn't my imagination playing tricks! We both heard him. It made me feel better about my own immortality. If a dog lives on, then surely human beings live on, too, after death.

~Mrs. William R., Michigan

TRIXIE & ZIPPY

My grandmother and I lived on a farm on Gobe Creek, West Virginia. For some fourteen years, we had a runty little dog – maybe part Rat Terrier –called Trixie. When she got old, she got extremely fat, almost helpless.

Trixie spent her days in cold weather lying before the gas heater in our dining room in the path from the kitchen to the front door. It had always been her favorite spot, and while she was agile and anyone came to the front porch, she would run to the door and bark. Trixie slept on the back porch in a box, and after she grew semi-helpless, we took her to it and covered her with a blanket. She slept outside until the next morning.

One morning after she had snored and struggled for breath so much it disturbed my study, I put my books down to go out, turn her over, and massage her head. The evening before, grandmother found her dead. I stayed home from school that day and we made a casket and buried Trixie by a cydonia tree in the garden. I carved her name on a stone block as her marker.

Grandfather had died a year or so before, after suffering with cancer. Sometimes we heard the sound of his slippers shuffling on the linoleum, and if we were in the dining room, Trixie would look up as if she saw him, and thump her tail. Sometimes she would even try to stand up as if to follow him.

After Trixie died, grandmother remarked that they were together again now, and rid of suffering. She took comfort from this thought.

From time to time, we would hear Trixie jump up from in front of the heater, and run to the door, her long nails clicking on the linoleum. She would bark in the living room. Sometimes someone would be on our porch. Sometimes, there would be no one whom we could see.

This persisted until we got another dog, Zippy, who looked part Chihuahua and part Corgi. He would not sleep in front of the heater, but raised his hair and barked at something he seemed to see lying there. If anyone came to the front door when he was in the kitchen he would run to the door, but would never go straight. Zippy would always detour around the spot where Trixie had lain. Once Zippy growled and snapped as he passed, flinching as if something had nipped at him.

We never saw anything, but sometimes we heard barking in the front room when Zippy was out in the yard. Other time we heard scratching at the back door, and Zippy would run in from the front room, bristling and growling and barking through the door. We peered through the window but saw nothing on the back porch.

Then one night when I was struggling with algebra, I heard Trixie struggling for breath on the screened porch. I realized I had been hearing it unconsciously for a long time. "Poor thing," I murmured, "I'd better go and turn her over." I arose before I realized Trixie had been dead for over two years, and that her box was in the loft over the grain house.

Zippy would not stay on the porch, and howled and kept up such a racket that grandmother brought him in and let him sleep on a chair by her bed the first night he was there. He would never sleep anywhere else after that.

Gooseflesh stood up all over me as I listened to the struggling breathing, and I woke grandmother and had her come and listen. She heard it also, and when I said, "I can't stand it here tonight with that going on," I said I'd turn the porch light on and see if the box and Trixie were visible.

She said, "No! Don't. You know we couldn't. We'd have seen her in front of the stove if we could see her like Zippy does."

"You think he sees her there?"

"Of course he sees her," she said. "Wait till it stops. If it's her death that we're hearing, it will stop."

After what seemed a very long time, it did stop, and grandmother sighed and said, "Dear God, let her be in peace. Let us be in peace. She is in your hands; let her rest." To me, she said, "Sleep in the middle room tonight if you don't want to sleep here." She went back to bed, and Zippy followed her to his chair.

I finally composed myself, and after hearing nothing more, I finally went to bed in my own room. Nothing disturbed me, and from that night on, we never heard Trixie again.

Zippy even began running to the door from the kitchen without worrying about the spot before the heater. After a while he eve began curling up in front of it himself.

I shall always believe we heard a repeat of the noise she made during her death struggle, which didn't wake me the night she died. I have no idea why such things should happen but these things did.

~Lee G., South Carolina

TIPPY

My son Paul was nine years old and the official owner of Tippy, a blue parakeet. He often rode on our shoulders or heads and was a busy, nosy little fellow. Twice I pulled him out of the goldfish bowl when he fell in while playing with the greenery.

We all loved him and were amused by his antics. He had a habit of flying rapidly through the house in a circle through the parlor, dining room, kitchen, the hall, and to the parlor again. His wings made a very distinctive whirring sound. When we heard him flying around in that way, we were all careful to keep clear because he went so fast.

Two years later, our five-year old daughter walked out the back door with Tippy on her shoulder. She didn't know he was there. He flew away and we couldn't get him back. Three days of nasty weather followed, so we had to assume Tippy was dead. We felt very sad.

That Christmas was a remarkable holiday where everyone was in tune and happy. After we opened gifts and had breakfast, I settled contentedly in the kitchen to wash dishes.

Suddenly Tippy flew through the kitchen making his rounds through the house twice.

We didn't see him, but the sound was unmistakable. My older daughter and I looked at each other and said, "Tippy just flew through here!" It made a good Christmas just perfect!

He never repeated the performance.

~Jean H., Ohio

CARAMEL

My dog Caramel had a freak accident with her hind legs. It took a month for her to die. She became progressively paralyzed, starting with the back legs and moving forward. At the end, all she was able to do was emit a hoarse bark.

I had Caramel on a lounge chair and I slept on the couch next to her. Each morning she would bark if I did not get up for work right away. For two days after she died, I still heard a hoarse bark. I was awake but had not gotten up yet. On the second day, I realized Caramel was still taking care of me.

I sat there and had a talk with her. I told her I loved her and didn't want her to hang around taking care of me. I wanted her to go on and do what she had to do. I told her I would manage.

That was the last I heard the bark.

~*Anonymous*, California

Sense

of

Sight

SENSE OF SIGHT

Our sense of sight is our visual perception and interpretation of the surrounding environment. The eyes see objects and our cognitive reasoning makes sense of what we see.

In this chapter and others, we go beyond the normal five senses and enter the realm of the sixth sense. This sense may cause us to question what we have seen and wonder whether it is real. If I indeed witnessed the reappearance of my pet, have other family members or household visitors seen the same thing? Is this a taboo subject? Will I face ridicule from others when discussing this matter?

These thought-provoking questions may leave you reevaluating your own sanity. However, the visual reappearance of a pet is more common than one may think.

Many people will never have an afterlife experience with their pet. Some pet owners may never see the spirit of their pet. This does not mean one person is more or less spiritual. This does not alter the love shared during the pet's lifetime.

I am not sure why some have these experiences and others do not, but we can hope to learn more from those who have already shared their encounters, and from those who will now be less fearful to share their own in the future.

FRECKLES AND THE GHOST

We had two small dogs, one male and one female. The female had a litter of puppies, but the daddy must have been the huge dog from across the street since the pups were very large. Only one survived birth. It was not long afterward I became aware of a fourth "dog" in the house.

I was sitting in the rocking chair reading in the living room and sensed a dog very near me. When I reached down to pet it, there was nothing there.

One night I woke up to see a dog's face inches from mine, but when I tried to pet it, it disappeared.

Another night, one of the dogs wanted to go out. I know I let three dogs out, but only two came back in. I waited quite a while, but the dog never showed up at the door. I finally checked the house and all three of our dogs were inside.

I had not said anything to my family about all this. My husband would have said I was nuts. I wasn't sure my son, who was eleven or twelve at the time, would understand either.

I was cleaning up after dinner when I asked my son to give Freckles (the male dog) a choice morsel that was left over. I knew the dog was outside near the back door. My son took it and headed for his bedroom instead. When I tried to tell him the dog was outside, he insisted he had seen Freckles sleeping in his room.

My son soon came back looking extremely puzzled. I had to explain to him he had met our ghost dog.

These incidents are the ones I remember most clearly, but the ghost dog was a continuous presence in my life for over two years. It all ended when the female dog next door got pregnant. I am convinced that when the puppies were born next door, our "ghost" was incarnated as one of them and disappeared from our lives. I really had grown fond of it and missed it.

~Lois H., Virginia

MAGICK?

The experience I had didn't concern my own pet. I had lived in a two-bedroom apartment for about ten months, and many times while I was there, I caught a glimpse of a cat running up the stairs or through the dining area.

At first I thought I was seeing things, but it happened so often I began to greet the creature on its appearances. It seemed to be a medium-sized cat, either black or grey with black stripes. It never approached me, but I would see it passing through as it were.

I told my boyfriend, but he scoffed at me. One evening he came over for dinner, and was seated at the dining room table. He glanced down casually and said, "Hi, Magick," the name of his own grey tabby cat.

He looked very startled as he realized we were not at his house. He looked up at me and I started to laugh. "See?" I admonished him. "I told you there was a ghost kitty here!" He was nervous the entire rest of the evening, but I felt vindicated.

I enjoyed having the cat around. It made me feel like I had company since we weren't allowed to have pets in those apartments. I don't know if it was someone's pet that got left behind, or someone's pet who had been happy there. It was a very harmless presence, and I certainly didn't mind sharing my home.

~Kathie T., California

BANDIT

I consider myself a reasonably sane person who does not pay much attention to psychic phenomena. I had a male American Cocker Spaniel named Bandit who had some behavioral problems. But he loved people and was great as long as things were going his way.

He was my constant companion and because of his behavioral problems, I got involved in dog training activities. I also bought the home I am now living in because it had a yard I could fence off for him. Eventually I went on to get four female Cocker Spaniels as well.

Bandit was a big factor in my retirement decision because I wanted to spend more time with him. Usually purchasing a dog is an impulsive decision, but somehow I believe I was guided by more than just fate to get this particular dog.

My wife and I have always had a dog in the family. As we were not blessed with children, dogs became our companions. We always had just one dog at a time until Bandit came along. We lost him at eight years old to continuing seizures.

He loved to stand on the stairs and survey his domain. After he passed on, I used to catch a glimpse of him just getting to the top steps passing to the bedroom. Sometimes my wife and I would be watching television, sitting on the sofa with our backs toward the stairs when the four dogs would look up and start barking.

I have heard a scratching at the back door and would get up to let a dog in. Except all four of ours were in the house when I checked.

I have awakened from a sound sleep and seen the black portion of Bandit's back passing by the foot of the bed. He has been gone four years now, but he is in my thoughts every day.

We have had and loved dogs in the past, but this particular dog was sent to change my life. He did. He has left now, but only temporarily. I believe in another time and place we will meet again.

~Clarence D., Maine

SIMON

The pet with whom I had the particular experiences is a male Red Point Siamese, aged seven weeks and one day when he died. His name was Simon. He died in my arms on May 11th after a very brief illness. To understand what happened, you have to keep in mind that I was totally and completely floored by his death. I suffered severe nervous breakdowns and was out of work for almost two years.

For four months following his death, both my roommate and I saw Simon as a small white form which would briefly appear in appropriate places. When he was alive Simon was mostly white, except for his "points", which were light peachy/apricot. Sometimes I saw him when my roommate wasn't nearby, and sometimes she saw him when I was away. He appeared by his kitty box. We had four other cats – that's why the litter box was still available. I would see Simon at the food and water dishes, on a little box he liked beside the toilet, and on the bed.

After we moved from the townhouse and the city where Simon died, my girlfriend never saw him appear again. But, upon arrival at our new apartment, I saw him once, by the cat food dishes in the kitchen. I never saw him there again, but I got the impression he was usually nearby. I felt good knowing he was near.

Still overcome with grief because of little Simon's death, I moved back home with my parents. I saw Simon two more times. He appeared on the bed briefly, perhaps just to let me know he was there.

The last time I saw him was on the second anniversary of his death. He was sitting in our flower bed about five feet away from his grave. I shouldn't say he was "sitting." It was more like a whitish flash hovered in the flowers.

~Laurie G., Canada

SHEILA

Shortly after we were married we got a German Shepherd/Collie mix puppy. She stayed with us through the birth and noise of four children. She would feel obligated to get up each and every time the baby cried and would guard the children most dutifully.

When Sheila was fourteen and a half, we had to move from one town to another. At that point she was past hearing and could barely see. She also had bladder problems. She wasn't happy, and regretfully I decided it was in her best interest to be put to sleep. It was a very hard decision. I loved her dearly.

My husband was out of state, and our two older children had moved on ahead of me. My two younger sons were with me in the house, but my youngest son was staying with a friend. Since I felt the child of seven was too young to be told, I didn't tell him beforehand. I brought Sheila and stayed with her myself.

Not letting my youngest son know beforehand turned out to be a bad choice. He and Sheila were close and he was inconsolable. We moved the next day and he would still cry at night for the dog.

After about a week of tears, I talked to him one morning and he told me he wouldn't cry any longer.

"Why?" I asked.

He said, "I don't have to anymore. Sheila came and told me goodbye last night. She said she is okay, and so I am, too."

"How do you know she came?"

"She jumped up on the bed, walked around, and laid down. I saw her."

I remembered Sheila's "tradition walk", or whatever you call it when dogs circle around before they lay down. She was a large dog, around eighty or ninety pounds. You definitely felt a jolt when she jumped on the bed. Her favorite place to sleep was with one of the kids.

I don't believe he actually saw the dog, rather saw the indentation of her steps and felt her fall asleep, but my son now corrects me and says he actually saw her.

If there was ever a dog that wouldn't want one of her kids to worry, it was Sheila.

I later saw her, too. I was on a swing-shift coming home about midnight down a big but deserted street when I saw her run cross the road. I came to a stop and was out of my car and called to her when she disappeared (and I realized she was dead). I strongly believe this happened for a reason – perhaps protection – but protection from what I will never know.

~Kathleen F., Colorado

JUDY

I had a white German Shepherd named Judy who I adored. She slept with me and ate with me. When she was nine and a half years old, she developed throat cancer. After two operations the vet advised me she should be put to sleep as she was in pain and soon wouldn't be able to eat. Very reluctantly I did this.

I lasted two days before I searched the area for another white Shepherd. Her name is Greta, and I am also devoted to her.

A year after Judy's death, I was enlisted to watch my grandchildren at night for two weekends while their mother went on a business trip. Since I had to sleep at their house, I told my companion to make sure he let the dogs out (I have two) before he went to bed.

When I returned the next day, he mentioned that Greta would not go out. He said he went into my room. She was lying on the bed and just lifted her head and stared at him when he tried to get her to go out. I asked if he was sure it was Greta, and he said yes.

This was impossible because at the last minute, I had decided to take Greta with me for the sleepover. She had been with me, in bed all night.

This other dog had been Judy, still lying in my bed and watching over me. This was very comforting.

~Maureen C., Massachusetts

Sense

of

Smell

SENSE OF SMELL

I believe every pet has a distinctive scent or odor that is pleasurable to the pet owner but not always to friends or family. Have you ever walked into someone else's house and smelled doggie odor or cats?

Your pet's special scent is recognizable to you, and is unique from all other pets. Certain toys, blankets, and pillows may retain the familiar scent. Other products like shampoo, pine bedding, hay, or pet food, may bring a special reminder of scents associated with your pet.

You know the scent of your pet, and can distinguish it from all others.

When hearing the phrase "sixth sense," most people think of extra-sensory perception or an individual with psychic abilities. Harvard researchers have discovered a specialized organ in the nose that produces a sixth sense capability[1].

This organ, the vomeronasal, senses chemicals called pheromones, secreted by animals and humans which are associated with emotions and instinct. Humans are able to identify these scents and associate the odor with conscious and unconscious past experiences. This recognition can have an effect on mood and behavior. Our nose is equipped with special sensors, making certain scents (such as the unique scent of our pets) easily identifiable.

---

[1] William J. Cromie. "Scientists Find Evidence for a Sixth Sense in Humans," *The Harvard University Gazette*, May 20, 1999.

MISSY

At almost twenty years of age, Missy's decline came suddenly, with rapid weight loss and weakness. The veterinarian agreed that as long as she was alert and eating well, and I was willing to care for her, Missy could have a little more time.

She had always been like a doting mother to me. Missy informed me when it was time to rise and time to go to bed. She let me know if I'd been out too long. She supervised my every chore, and when I was ill, she would curl up on my pillow with her arms around my neck. Every evening she lay on my chest.

Now I was the doting mother. I fed her by hand, groomed her, and carried her to and from the litter box. I kept her against my chest or on a hot water bottle night and day. I prepared myself for her death the only way I knew how.

I prepared a box covered with rose-print paper and lined it with soft white flannel. I put a lock of my hair and a sketch of myself with Missy and other pets inside. I searched the linen closet for something to cover her body. All my towels were matched sets except for one: a nice little rose-pink hand towel.

I had arranged everything with my veterinarian for when the time came to have Missy put down. But on that day, my own vet was away. Having never had to put an animal to sleep before, I was not aware there was a right way and a wrong way. I wanted Missy to go peacefully, knowing how much she was loved. The attending vet made the whole ordeal painful and traumatic.

After it was all over, I placed her in the little box, covered her with the rose-colored towel, sealed the box, and a dear friend of mine buried her for me.

For weeks I mourned, plagued with guilt about the way she spent her last few moments. I was inconsolable.

One day I reached into the linen closet for clean towels, and there, folded neatly on top, was the same towel I had covered Missy with.

Several days later, while sitting on the sofa, I noticed a lovely floral scent. Every time I sat on the sofa I noticed that scent. Visitors would also notice and comment on that scent.

One day a dear friend and well-known psychic told me the towel and scent were Missy's way of letting me know she was still around

It was then I noticed the scent was emanating from the area of my left shoulder and chest – Missy's favorite resting spot. At that point, the beautiful smell left and has not returned.

The rose-colored towel, however, is with me still.

~Louis T., Canada

VERA

For over three years, I had an extraordinary pet named Vera. She was a Savannah Monitor Lizard given to me when she was just a baby.

The first year and a half I had her, she was pretty feisty and intimidated me. I was tentative when reaching into her cage to get her. By the time she was around two years old though, and over thirty inches long, we had developed quite a bond between us. There was trust on both our sides.

She became my unique friend and was an eager face waiting for me when I came home from work. People say reptiles do not love, and I'm sure that's true for some, but it was very clear that Vera held an incredible amount of love for me. She loved receiving that love back in return. She was my baby.

After two months of battling suspicious symptoms, many trips to the vet, and a great deal of in-home care, I lost Vera to cancer and liver disease. The morning she died, I held her head in the palm of my hand until she just slipped away. At that point, I just wanted her to drift off to sleep because I was afraid she was hurting. I wanted the suffering to stop. And so she did. I loved her so much, and at the time, I just couldn't believe this little treasure was gone.

For the next two hours I held her. I touched her and examined every part of her face. Vera possessed a wonderful, sweet smell, and as I sat there holding her, I breathed in this aroma repeatedly, as deeply as possible. I savored every second until I finally had to give her back to the earth.

Ten days after Vera's death, I was working at the dental office. It was an extremely busy, non-stop day. The type of day that allows you only to think about the next patient coming in and finding a way to get ready for them when you have ten other things going on all at the same time.

I had been assisting the doctor in one operatory, took off my latex gloves, and left the room to go prepare another operatory for another patient. I had just walked in this one room, began cleaning it up, and recognized a familiar scent.

In a second, I knew it was Vera. It immediately grew stronger and stronger. My first thought was to wonder what it was and where it was coming from. Within a minute, it was as I was holding her right in my hands. The scent was that vivid and close. I looked down at my hands and for a moment wondered if it was from wearing the latex gloves (not that I'd ever noticed it before). I brought my hands to my face and inhaled. The smell was so strong, almost exaggerated. I was so shaken with emotion I started to cry right there.

I *had* to get the room cleaned up though, and was trying to regain my composure. It was hard to move. I stood there and breathed in all in, inhaling with my deepest of breaths. It was so emotionally disturbing but at the same time intoxicating.

The scent was *on* my hands or it was *in* my hands. Not a similar smell, but I was *experiencing* it. I stood in that room for about four minutes. I managed to get it cleaned and prepared for the next patient, but the whole time I was so shaken up and wanted to cry. It was so real. She was there. But she wasn't. It was confusing and painful.

I went to the sterilization area, continually sniffing my hands, and by the time I had been in that area for just a few seconds, the scent began to fade. I hated for it to go. It faded fast, then the whole experience was over. My hands went back to smelling like latex and powder. The operatory smelled no different than normal, just like a dentist's office.

I will never forget this experience. Once the painful emotional part was over, I felt so incredibly touched. So fortunate. So blessed.

Without a doubt, I know Vera visited me that day. It was a most unbelievable, unforgettable event in that five minutes.

I am so grateful that now I have had a true experience to confirm there is life after life, and true love and friendship are everlasting and ever-present. When two souls join, they can never be parted.

~Donna E., Washington

TINY

We raised this all-black Dachshund from six weeks to twelve years, until we had Tiny put to sleep after the vet assured us there was no hope.

My husband said I'd murdered her and I felt badly enough without hearing that. He built a solid wood casket, which took most of a day, and we buried her out back with a marker for her grave – much nicer than many babies, so we have been told. We grieved so much for her as she was a part of our household.

One evening, I was lying on the davenport watching television. I felt a warm body under my arm and it felt solid, exactly like Tiny used to do when either of us would be lying down there. I told my husband immediately, but he scoffed and said it was my imagination. Shortly after this happened, the same thing happened to him – only this time, he believed.

Another night we both saw a black form come through the living room door and lie on the throw rug. This was another one of her favorite places.

I must add that before Tiny died, she had a peculiar odor we'd never smelled before.

Two years later, we bought a large home seventeen miles from our present location. Soon after we moved in, I was lying in the living room. A black form walked across the room, but not before I'd smelled the odor. This odor was present many times.

I said to my husband that Tiny just wants us to know she still loves us. I thought it meant it was time for us to stop grieving for her. I think deep grief may keep the dead from going on to a higher plane. Anyway, after we stopped talking so much about her and stopped grieving, we never had any other occurrences.

~Maxine W., Ohio

Sense

of

Touch

SENSE OF TOUCH

The sense of touch is the perception of objects, shape, weight, temperature and texture received by the conscious mind. When it comes to our pets we notice the texture of their fur, their wet nose on our face and the lick of their tongue on our body. We notice the warmth and comfort of their bodies pressed up against ours.

A cat may dig its claws into the owner's foot if disturbed while sleeping at the end of the bed. Some owners feel the weight and touch of a dog or cat landing on the bed. Pets might have a distinctive way they press their nose against the owner's face, or a special kiss on the lips.

The weight of a 110-pound dog lying across you may feel as though a car landed on top of you. The pulling strain of a leash wrapped around your hands when another dog approaches is a common feeling pet owners may experience. The doorbell ringing and your dog barrelling past you on the stairs like a herd of elephants almost knocking you off balance can make you feel like you lost the race.

These sensations are individual and specific. You know the unique characteristics of your pet's touch.

TOMASINA

I wasn't going to write to you at first. I'd never told anyone about what happened. I thought I was crazy. I had an old cat, Tomasina, who slept with me every night in the same positions – curled up either between my feet or behind my knees – depending on how I was sleeping.

She was over twenty years old and still frisky until the day before she died. I held her in my arms when the vet gave her the final shot.

I really missed my "bed buddy" at night and mentioned to people I missed sleeping with a cat.

Several weeks later, I awoke during the night and tried to get out of bed. I couldn't throw the covers back because "the cat" was sleeping there. There was definitely a cat-sized something laying on the blanket over my feet.

I told her to move and went to push her over when I remembered Tomasina had passed. Suddenly the pressure was gone. I know I was awake at the time. The experience didn't scare me. I felt oddly comforted by it.

It happened many more times over the next several weeks. Each time I didn't move or talk. I just enjoyed the company. One time I did move my foot though. She dug her claws into my foot just like she always did. She hated to be disturbed!

~B. A. B., Massachusetts

GEMINI

In January, I lost a very special and dear cat, Gemini. I brought her up from a five-week old abandoned kitten the vet said couldn't survive. Survive she did, and she was almost human.

She saw me through some good and sad times and we were very close. I talked to her as I do to my five present cats. When she died at age ten, I was grief stricken. Even as I write this, the memories of her make me weep. In time I went through the three phases of grief. My experience has been in spirit I think.

Many times I have sat on the bed or sofa and have felt the touch of a cat land on the bed behind me. When I turn to welcome one of my cats, there is nothing there. After this happened several times, I mentioned it to one of my daughters. As if she read my mind she said, "Do you suppose it was Gemini?" There was no other explanation.

Gemini came to visit many times until a year ago March. From the time I lost her, I kept looking for another calico – every time I thought I had found one it was taken. This went on for ten months. I had given up finding a calico – they are hard to find here in Florida.

A gorgeous black-and-white stray came into my life. She was pregnant and was about to be given to the Humane Society. Although I am only allowed two cats in my apartment, I said I couldn't let this cat go, and I took her in and hid her. I planned on finding a home for the whole bunch later.

My two cats took to her and we fell in love with her. When the kittens arrived, there were three calicos, one gray and one brown tabby.

My daughter who shares the apartment with me decided to adopt the classic brown tabby. When she had lived in Iowa, my daughter had been too late to save a similar cat from freezing to death after it had been abandoned. She never forgot that poor thing, and so she loved this new kitten dearly.

I picked one of the calicos without any big decision between the three. We found great, loving homes for the others and keep in touch with the owners.

The calico I picked does everything the way Gemi did. It's amazing. Even people and family have noticed the very same and unusual traits. "Just like Gemi," they say.

I think Gemi came back in my Lulu. She is a calico and the fur and coloring are not the same at all, but there is something especially familiar about her!

~E. Gloria T., Florida

FLASH

When I was in my teens, I had a horse I loved very much. I didn't own him, but for five beautiful years I rode and cared for him. Then I got married and moved away. I never forgot Flash, and a year later my husband and I came to visit him. Much to my horror and sorrow, he had to be put to sleep because of an illness. We were going to buy him. You can't imagine how I felt that day.

Anyway, fifteen years went by. I never for a moment forgot my horse or the way I let him down. I was living in New Jersey, It was a bitter cold, but sparkling bright winter morning. I decided to take a walk.

As I walked I began thinking of days like that one when I use to ride Flash, and how beautiful my horse used to look in the sun, and how I still wished he were with me. Suddenly I felt a warm soft breath on my cheek. I knew then, and I know today, it was my horse. He always laid his nose against my cheek in affection. I felt it, soft and warm, only for a few seconds, but it was there. The day was so cold, below zero.

For a long time I kept placing my hand upon my cheek. I was amazed and a little afraid. It was real. It happened. It wasn't much, but it was everything to me. I swear it to be true.

I have been laughed at so I don't talk about it anymore. But it was a very wonderful thing, and I know wherever my beautiful horse is, he is thinking of me also.

Recently I had to lose a dog I loved very much. She has been gone five months and I still miss her terribly. I have not seen or felt anything. But somehow I know the two are with me every day.

~Barb W., Pennsylvania

BOXER AND SIAMESE EXPERIENCE

When I was about seven or eight years old, our neighbor had a Boxer named Honey who fell off the fire escape and died. That night when I went to sleep my arm was dangling off the bed and I swear I felt Honey lick my hand.

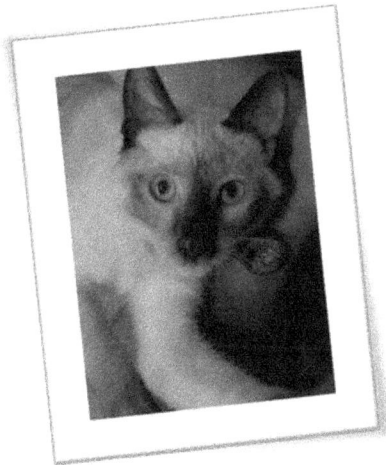

As a teenager, I had a beautiful Seal Point Siamese kitten. She was about ten weeks of age when she died. When I went to bed that evening I felt her walk by the top of my head, as I lay on the pillow, and settle down to sleep. I had the feeling she was alright and comfortable.

~Madeline B., New York

BOBBI

My second dog was a Brittany Spaniel named Bobbi. We had her several years. She was overweight so the vet insisted she be put on a drastic diet. This changed her a bit – she began looking everywhere for anything edible. She killed a rabbit for the first (and only) time.

Bobbi became ill. She couldn't keep food down and had diarrhea. We later came to believe she had eaten poison put out by a neighbor to kill a wild creature in our rural area, or perhaps she found some rotted mass in one of the leaf piles we use for the garden.

The doctor gave her a blood transfusion and predicted her recovery hours before she died. It was a sad thing to watch her drain away. Mama said she went to check on Bobbi after our dinner. The dog looked up at her as if to say "I'll be OK" and then fell asleep dead. We were upset, to say the least.

My fiancé and I were in the final hectic stages of plans for a large party that next weekend. I felt Bobbi's loss but not as much as the week after the party when I had no planning to occupy my mind. I'd just about gotten over the whole thing in three weeks.

One night I came home alone. Mama and Papa were upstairs waiting for me. I unlocked the rec room door with my key, pushed it open and was immediately greeted by a dog jumping on me.

I froze, thinking Mama and Papa had surprised me with a new dog so soon after Bobbi. I reached for the light and turned it on hurriedly to see this new dog. There was nothing but an empty room. I am convinced Bobbi greeted me that night.

We all felt a strange presence of her that week – as if she returned to tell us she was okay. The presence left, although occasionally we hear sounds as if she were there. The sounds could be in our memories, but the greeting was not. I wasn't scared by it but I was shaken, particularly since I felt her but could see nothing.

I haven't entered that door alone after dark since. I'm living in my own apartment now with my third dog. We visit all the time and there is no negative feeling towards him so I guess if Bobbi is watching over the place she accepts him.

~Brittany Spaniel Lover, Pennsylvania

SPRITE

We purchased Sprite at a pet shop one summer. He was a perfect Cockapoo (3/4 Poodle). I found he had a birthday exactly one week after mine, and it made me feel special.

Sprite and I became inseparable friends. Even while away at school, he waited for me. My mother always remarked how Sprite would "know" I was on my way home, regardless if I was late or early.

When we moved, Sprite felt at home in the new house immediately. For the first time in his life, he knew what it was like to run up stairs!

Sprite had only one fault, for he was a free spirit, and enjoyed running and running. This got him in trouble several times. Anytime my parents wanted to punish him, he hid under my bed. Whenever I was under some kind of attack (verbally or kiddingly) he would always defend me.

Shortly after we moved, I came across a kitten at school – a tiny, dainty Tortoiseshell kitten, part Siamese. Tansy and Sprite became fast friends, chasing each other around, wrestling, and cleaning each other.

That spring, Sprite ran off. His dog friend across the street had died and possibly Sprite ran just to get away from it all. One afternoon our neighbors found him on the side of the road having been struck by a car. Sprite had almost made it home. I cried for over a month. My parents called him a good-for-nothing dog and said I shouldn't carry on so. But it just made it worse. They still don't understand.

That same year, I lost Sprite, Tanzy, and our old family tomcat Hicckey, too. My parents gave away all the kittens, and I felt so miserable I felt like killing myself. My only consolation was Scooter.

Scooter was born in May, two months after Sprite's demise and on what would have been his third birthday. There were many strange things surrounding his birth. Besides being apricot-colored and born on my dog's birthday, he is an 'only' kitten – a litter of one. Tanzy got the name Momma-Cat for fawning over him so much.

Sprite had been an only puppy and was evidently fawned over by his mother and former owner. When we bought him at eight weeks old, he had just had a haircut and smelled of talcum powder.

Scooter soon grew into a fat, small kitten. When the Momma-Cat had four kittens, he nursed with them, despite the fact he was three months older.

One week prior, Hicckey died of natural causes. I found out later he had saved Momma-Cat's soon to be kittens.

That Thanksgiving, Tanzy died of rat poisoning. She wasn't quite two years old. Even to this day Scooter goes in the basement and meows for his mother and the kittens. Thank goodness Scooter is still here! Scooter growls like a dog and follows me around like a puppy, his tail swinging from side to side.

These "feelings" began last summer. Lying in bed, I heard something walk across the bedroom floor and lay down in the corner with a sigh. More than once Scooter has walked into my room, growled and walked out.

The strangest feelings came a few months ago, during Christmas vacation. I was lying in bed, trying to get to sleep, when I heard that familiar walking noise. It went to the foot of my bed, and then I felt little feet walking across the bed. They stopped, curled up in a ball, and the animal began to clean itself. I could feel the warmth against my legs, and unclasped toenails digging into the comforter. It was Sprite.

For about half an hour I laid there, listening to his cleaning noises, grunts, and sighs. I finally moved my leg, and the feeling vanished. Scooter had been out the entire night, and was not let in until the next morning.

Every once and a while the feeling will come back, a funny warmth against my leg, and sometimes, a smaller one will accompany him.

Tanzy? I think so.

~Andrea G., Michigan

GEMENI

We had a male Siamese Seal Point which my wife had for fifteen years. The cat had been suffering and was losing weight. After taking it to the vet we found Gemeni had severe kidney failure. Reluctantly we had him put to sleep.

We both cried as we loved this extremely gentle cat which I nicknamed "Gentle Ben." Gemeni had a habit of climbing onto my lap while I was watched television. I would realize I had been petting him ten or fifteen minutes later without remembering he had been in my lap.

Our antique business took us on the road for four or five weeks at a time. We used an airstream travel trailer, and our four cats all got along great and enjoyed running as a pack and traveling in our trailer. Two days after Gemeni died, we had to leave on a four-week trip.

At night all the cats would sleep on the bed with us. Gemeni had a particular habit of only getting up on the bed when we both were in it. Then he always got up at the right-hand corner at the foot of the bed. We always knew it was him.

The first night on the road we went to bed. The three remaining cats were on the bed with us when we felt the corner of the bed depress. We could feel walking on the bed toward us as if Gemeni had just jumped up on the bed. My wife and I were both awake and we both at the same time commented to each other that it felt like Gemeni had jumped on the bed and walked toward us.

I immediately turned on the light and we saw the other three cats laying together on the far side of my wife. All three of them were alert and looking at a depression on the other side of me where it had felt like Gemeni had jumped up, walked over, and laid down.

My wife and I felt Gemeni had actually done this and the other cats were looking at the spot. She and I started to talking to him, telling him we loved him so much and that he would always be welcome to come and visit us. We both felt he heard us and understood we loved and missed him.

I felt the spot on the bed and it was warm. It made the hair stand up on my arms. The other cats walked over and smelled the spot.

Gemeni still stands out in my mind as the most gentle and loving cat I have ever known. To this day I am convinced he came back to say goodbye.

~Len B., Florida

PRINCESS

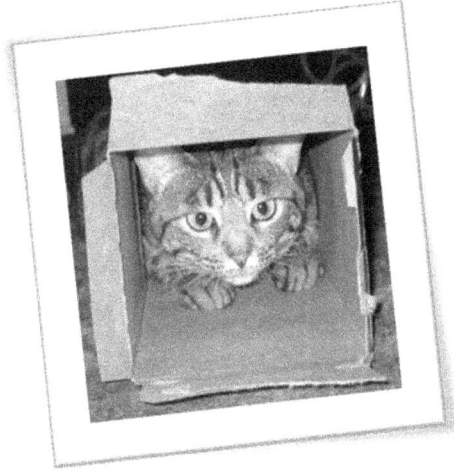

For a number of years I would go to bed at night and feel my cat Princess jump on my bed. I would look for her but she would not be there. I would call her and she would come. I would sometimes feel the jumping on the bed and walking on it, but my cat would already be on the bed asleep prior to the jump.

At one time I really thought I was going nuts and would sometimes kid with my friends telling them I must have a ghost cat living with me. One of my friends thought it might be a human ghost and that I could not tell the difference between the two.

After several years, I acquired several more cats and stopped letting them into my bedroom. But the jumping onto the bed continued. I also noticed on my cats acting funny on several occasions. I would see one or the other starring into empty space and then swiping at that space with their paws. Or one would play hide and seek with thin air.

Once we had a severe storm of hurricane strength. I just sat at one end of the couch, hoping to keep my cats as calm as possible. Within a few minutes I felt something jump onto the couch next to me. I sat very still and watched.

Within a few seconds, my red smoke Persian-Cameo "Tammy," who is very jealous, opened her eyes and looked over. She stared at the spot next to me, came over and started meowing. All of a sudden I felt movement and jumping off – like a little weight was removed from the couch. Tammy started to follow something I could not see. She used her paws as if to pat at something, and then started playing the old peek around the corners of the coffee-table bit.

I thought that by now, not only I had lost my marbles, but that my cats were going bananas, too.

Shortly after this event, I had the chance to go to a very good medium and was told I had a small dog spirit living with me. The description fitted my very first dog Bobby. He was a miniature Spitz, which would account for the weight jumping on the bed and couch.

I had owned Bobby when I still resided in West Germany and he died of double pneumonia when I was a young girl. He was my dog though and I was very upset for a long time after he died.

So, you can see even thousands of miles make no difference to a free spirit. He has not been in my house now for about two years.

~Ruth H., New Jersey

Other Pets

Recognize

The Departed

OTHER PETS RECOGNIZE THE DEPARTED

Since people have existed on earth, we have had special relationships to the animals around us. Space anthropologists believe there were two basic interests that early man had in animals: hunting them for food or other life support needs and endowing them with symbolic powers in order to develop magical or religious beliefs.

By the time civilizations were established, animals played important roles. The selected animals were either deities or possessed the magical powers to foretell the future. Ancient Egyptians deified the cat and gave magical powers to the crocodile. Later on, Moses condemned the Jewish people who built and worshipped the golden calf. This worship of animals was a constant weakness in the ancient Israelite nation which the Old Testament prophets constantly condemned and warned of God's judgment for doing such things. In ancient Greece and Rome, doves and lambs were sacrificed and their internal organs examined by the priests or priestesses in order to predict events for individuals or the nation.

Today, animals do not hold such magical powers in the Western or industrial cultures, especially where sophisticated religious beliefs exist, but there are still primitive and certain Eastern religions where animals hold godlike powers. Western nations mostly use animals for symbolic purposes.

Wherever there is mankind, there is going to be folklore about the powers and the symbolic nature of animals. For example, Europeans originally saw the swan as a symbol of death. Just as this one animal represented death, other animals served as symbols for the idea of resurrection in other cultures and these animals include the swan (certain Asian cultures), the peacock and the fish.

No matter how sophisticated a society may be, animals are still used to represent symbolic ideas. These symbolic ideas are not just confined to the area of religion.   In our society, who does not know the symbolic power of the bear (Russian government) or the eagle (American government)? The money that we use carries the symbolic image of the eagle.

Animals, whether as pets or symbols, have an impression on our thinking. We may even venture to say that it Is impossible to go through a whole month without talking to someone else about some type of animal.

In our modern age, people have reported changes in animal behavior prior to an earthquake, though the people themselves never knew anything was about to happen. Also, scientists have documented how certain animals, notably porpoises and elephants, protect one of their kind who is incapacitated or dying. Elephants have been photographed fondling the bones of a former elephant, giving the appearance of the human qualities of inquisitiveness and sadness.

Obviously, as scientists study the ways of animals, we have to respect them for their individual uniqueness and not think of them as only dumb creatures who eat, sleep and die.

Just as people have noted that animals can often predict earthquakes, some pet owners have observed their pets reacting to what seems to be a pet apparition.

The skeptic might dismiss all animal behavior as an easily explainable conditioning experience. Thus a skeptic might propose that a pet is not really reacting to a "ghost" but is following very subtle or unconscious conditioning signals from the despondent owner. The skeptic believes the pet is reacting in an unusual manner as the owner would want it to react.

Can every ADPP experience be so simply explained? How can we explain the unusual actions of elephants around an elephant skeleton, considering they are not doing anything in their actions to "please" any human being? How can we explain the "powers" of some animals to detect a coming earthquake? Is there anything of a psychic ability which we could learn from the animals? Furthermore, why do some animals react so fearfully to an apparent pet apparition and then - suddenly - their behavior is completely normal the rest of their lives?

We will begin to look at the following accounts and let you try to make up your mind about these possible ADPP experiences.

BENTLY

About two years ago, my daughter's huge, fat, grey tabby cat was killed by a truck. Kathy loved her cat Bently more than any other we have owned. She was due to go into the Air Force three months after Bently was killed.

We received a Ouija board for Christmas that year, and as Kathy was very much still mourning Bentley's death, we tried to contact him. Slowly, the letters spelled out, "Goodbye, Kathy."

That really made her day as she felt somehow, in that other world where animals go, Bentley said goodbye to the mistress he loved so much. To this day she still mourns her great grey tabby who held such a special place in her heart.

~Lou M., California

CRYBABY, PATCHES, & HEIDI

A friend and I were mutually interested in the supernatural and occult. A waitress who worked in his restaurant owned an absolutely notorious haunted house which she inherited from her foster parents. My friend thought I would like to meet this young lady and tour the house.

You could write an epic volume on the general psychic phenomena in the house, let alone the animal experiences. So late one August night, my friend telephoned her at his restaurant and made arrangements.

The house itself was a disappointment – nondescript red brick bungalow of late 1920's vintage, typical of tens of thousands built in the Chicago area in that era.

After being introduced to Chris and her fiancé, I settled down in the living room to converse with them. Two large cats, Crybaby (a golden feline) and Patches (a spotted black and white, with seven toes on each front paw!) and a young German Shepherd, Heidi, played on the braided rug before us by the fireplace. Chris proceeded to the kitchen to fix us coffee and midnight snacks.

In telling me about the phenomena that had gone on in the house, young Roland (Chris's fiancé) produced a color photograph that had been taken in the house several weeks before. It showed the fireplace with its typical 1920's flanking glass-enclosed built-in bookcases, with a ghostly hand reflected in one glass bookcase panel, pointing at a particular book.

Roland then produced the book. It was a teenage girl's Nancy Drew-type mystery book, with a page showing a duplicate ghostly hand pointing in the same gesture to a pier where a character had drowned!

On further examination of the photo, I noted the two cats and the dog also appeared in it. Patches and Heidi stretched out lazily before the fireplace, but the golden cat, Crybaby, stood facing the camera with eyes blazing and every hair on her back standing up.

Later, while I was alone in the living room, just as the clock struck midnight, Crybaby sprang three feet off the braided rug where she had been dozing. Without taking a forward leap, she flew straight up in the air with every hair on her back standing up.

I yelled for Chris who was in the kitchen, "Come see what your cat is doing!"

After rushing into the living room and hearing my explanation, she casually dismissed it with, "Oh, that. She does that all the time, right about midnight."

On subsequent visits to the house, I would sit in the living room in a comfortable lounge chair, with one or both cats dozing contentedly in my lap while I stroked them. All of a sudden, from the very picture of peace and contentment, they would jump out of my lap and walk stealthily toward the large double entranceway to the dining room.

They hissed and snarled viciously, with every hair standing up straight on their backs, and peered into a dark corner of the unlit dining room. They never crossed the floor sill that divided the two rooms.

The pup, however, seemed totally immune to the psychic presences that were all over the house. Chris told me that while the cats reacted violently and fearfully to the footsteps in the hall, locked doors that opened and closed by themselves, and the old Remington typewriter in a back bedroom that would suddenly start typing by itself, Heidi showed no reaction whatsoever.

~Robert D., Tennessee

155

BUNJIE & THE COCKER

I went to the cleaners one day after work, first picking up my dog from home so she could accompany me. While I was inside the store, my miniature poodle Bunjie waited in the car parked right outside. The cleaners had huge picture windows enabling me to clearly see my dog.

As I was paying my bill, a pickup truck pulled alongside the window, blocking my view of Bunjie. She began barking wildly. At first, I was slightly irritated with the truck because I could no longer "see" my dog. Then I noticed a blond Cocker Spaniel looking out the side window of the truck and my irritation ceased.

The dog was running back and forth from the window closest to Bunjie to the window closest to the cleaners. I knew Bunjie was having a fine time "talking" with the Cocker Spaniel so I thought no more about it.

I left the cleaners and was putting my cleaning in my car when the owner of the truck came out. He said, "That's a cute dog you have there."

I thanked him and let him know I thought his dog was adorable, too.

"Why, I don't have a dog!" he replied.

I told him I had seen a dog in his truck just as clearly as I was seeing him right then. However, when I looked at his truck there was no dog's face looking out. I was in total disbelief! I asked again if he was sure he didn't have a dog.

He said he did not and added that his dog had died a couple of months before.

I asked the man what kind of dog it was and he said it was a Cocker Spaniel.

"A blonde one?" I asked.

He said his dog had been blonde, in fact, kind of golden.

I shared with him all I had seen and that the dog looked very alert and healthy.

I never saw the man again but I know we both left the cleaners that day believing that somehow, for whatever reason, that little Cocker Spaniel's spirit was traveling happily with its master.

Although the man had shared some details of the dog's age and cause of death, I have forgotten them. I do remember the man and dog were closely bonded. I will never forget that cute blonde face looking out that window at me. There is no doubt in my mind what I encountered was deeply spiritual.

~Linda S., Michigan

SHADOW CAT

My family moved into an 1890's house in Falls Church, Virginia. Although unusual happenings occurred, I was inclined to dismiss most of them to the character of the house. However, a shadow of a cat would appear at many points, such as at the top of either of the staircases. When approached, it would turn and leave – as any cat not wishing to be picked up. It would then vanish, leaving no trace in either the hallway, nor any room. This happened in sight of most of my family, including my highly skeptical father.

During the seven-year period we lived in the house, we owned several cats of our own, as well as a small mixed Terrier. Our pets would sometimes romp with our shadowy spirit. Once, and I shall never forget, our dog chased the phantom up the hall, and into my room. Disquietingly, it seemed to pass over my very feet, disappearing into an adjoining room. The dog only stopped in her tracks, and looked questioningly from the room to me.

The only indication we ever had as to the identity of the spirit was the skeleton of a cat found amid the clutter in the large barn behind the house. Trunks and papers were there dating from the original owners.

When we first moved in, we owned a female mixed Persian kitten, and a large tiger-striped tom. Illya (the male) raised the kitten, C.J., who had been taken from her mother prematurely. With the babying she received from all of us, C.J. remained very childlike. When another cat would enter our yard, Illya would "escort" C.J. to the safety of our back porch, and leave her in sanctuary while he defended his domain.

We always brought them in for the night. They usually returned home for themselves or when called. One night Illya did not respond, He had been struck by a car and killed, having been tempted across the street to chase moles in a newly cleared lot. My brother retrieved the body, and wrapped it in plastic and heavy blankets.

He dug a grave more suitable for a person than a cat, and buried the beloved pet. We covered the grave with stones and leaves. Even with many animal smells about (squirrel, chipmunk, and birds), C.J. would sit and sleep upon Illya's grave continually.

Other pets we adopted would only divert her attention away from the grave for a short time. The spirit cat had already been about, and Illya had chased it.

~*Anonymous*, Idaho

SAM

Last year we lost our German Shepherd, Sam, and mourned him as one would any other family member. At intervals since then, both my husband and I often hear his step on the porch and the characteristic swat he used to give the screen door when he wanted to come in.

Our three other Shepherds, who were all in the house with us, prick up their ears but do not bark. Any out-of-the-ordinary sound always touches off a salvo of barking.

~E. M., California

PSYCHIC CHIHUAHUA

My mother-in-law had a Chihuahua a few years back. It was an obnoxious little thing! I couldn't stand the dog because if you even looked at him he'd bite so I never touched him or even petted him.

My husband's grandmother was seriously ill in the hospital. I was around five months pregnant and we had stopped at my in-laws one night after leaving the hospital. We were sitting around the table when her little dog came up to me and started to cry and howl. The dog then jumped up on my lap, and kept howling and giving his paw.

I put him down on the floor and he jumped on me again. This kept up until we left and he tried to go home with me. That night Grandma died. I still think that dog was trying to tell us something.

What I still can't understand was that for six and a half years I could never go near that dog and the night Grandma died I could have taken the Chihuahua anywhere or done anything to him. He wouldn't leave me alone the whole evening. As fast as I put him down on the floor he was back up again.

~ Donna R., Pennsylvania

GHOST CAT

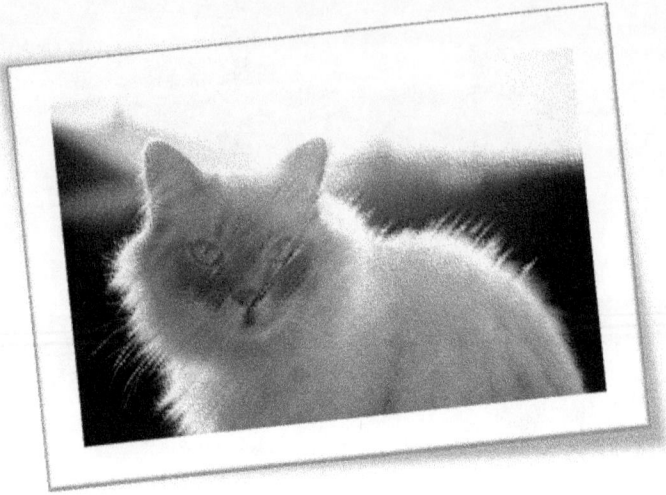

We are a normal family of four. Nothing special. My husband and I have been to college and have been married for nine years.

For the last seven years, we have lived peacefully with a pet ghost. Our pet is a cat and was already there when we moved into our house. His place seems to be the hall, although he does come into the older part of our kitchen.

Our own dogs don't seem to notice him, but both our cats arch their backs and spit at him. He almost looks real, and I have walked around him several times while housecleaning. His eyes even shine in the dark like live animals' eyes.

~Patricia Y., New York

Dreams

&

Reality

DREAMS & REALITY?

Maybe you've woken from a vivid dream and were convinced it was real. I believe there may be truth in our dreams about daily awake events. In dreams our brain can process events and situations, looking for solutions.

Once I dreamed about a cat being terrorized by another cat. I woke and got into the car. I drove randomly, being led by some other force. I ended up about seven miles from home at the end of a road in an unfamiliar neighborhood. A black cat was attacking a young kitten. I drove my van closer and flashed my high beams. The black cat took off. The kitten seemed okay but I couldn't fathom how I received this message.

I had another vivid dream of my brother who was about to go fishing in Ocean City, Maryland, with a friend. They got into an argument with another boater and he pulled a knife out on him. I warned him to be careful and told him about the dream. While on his fishing trip another boater got very close to theirs and ran his motor across their fishing line and rigs. A big argument ensued that almost went to fisticuffs.

Nothing prepares us for the loss of a pet or loved one. Unexplainable things happen in this world all the time but we know things happen that are more than mere coincidence. I enjoy investigating the unexplained happenings only to seek answers to the truth about living and dying.

ROCKY

Rocky, a salt-and-pepper Miniature Schnauzer, came to live with us when he was ten weeks old. He was the first dog my husband and I had since married, though we were both raised with dogs.

Sadly, Rocky did not grow up to be an ideal companion animal. He was very aggressive with visitors and almost every dog we met on walks. He had bitten several people by the time we sought professional intervention.

After consulting three different vets and two behaviorists, we decided to have Rocky euthanized. We came to this very painful decision because we were concerned for the safety of our one-year old daughter. We tried to find another home for Rocky, and had tried every other training method and drug therapy of which we were aware, but nothing provided us with sufficient improvement. We actually did find a new home for him, but it lasted only two days.

I was not prepared for the pain of grief I would suffer once he was gone. I can honestly say I cried on and off for six months after Rocky left us. I would be driving in the car on my way home from work, and thoughts of him would pop into my head. I would burst into almost uncontrollable tears. I used to wish the vet hadn't really gone through with the euthanasia but had rather tricked us into thinking he had so I might see Rocky alive once again.

One evening while driving home from work, I was stricken with another fit of grief. I asked out loud to see him again. Just one more time. To hold him and feel his soft fur against my face.

As the evening wore on, I snapped out of it and forgot about my earlier episode. I put my daughter to bed and a little while later, my husband and I retired for the evening.

That night I had a dream that was so real I am still not sure it was really a dream. In it, I saw Rocky and he looked wonderful. He came running to me with a big smile on his face and told me he was okay. I told him how much I longed to hold him just one more time. I could feel him and smell him just the way he had been when he was alive. It felt wonderful.

When I woke the next morning, I remembered everything very vividly and still had a feeling that it wasn't a dream at all. It felt so real.

From that night on, the grieving has stopped. I know Rocky understood that my husband and I did what we thought was the right things for everyone involved. There was no animosity in him toward us when I saw him that night – only and abundance of love and consolation.

~Rose R., New York

CAREY

My friend, Crystal, was a very special person to a lot of people. Her kind and loving ways with people and animals gained much love and respect from all who came to know her.

Crystal was driving home from a dog show when a drunk ran two stop signs and hit her car. She was killed instantly. With her was a sixteen-year old poodle that was deaf and blind. Crystal had picked her up to take her along at the last moment. The little old dog was killed also, but her beautiful Golden Retriever escaped and was lost 200 miles from home.

I took a friend and we did locate the dog and returned him to a stunned and grieving family.

Soon after Crystal's death, my beloved Belgian was killed. It was a sudden and senseless accident and I felt responsible. My grief was so depressing I couldn't pull myself out of it. I couldn't talk to anyone about it as no one would understand such grief for a dog. I heard his bark constantly and every glimpse of a big red dog sent me running to look for him.

One night I dreamed my husband and I were driving along a peaceful country road searching for the dog and saw a lady coming down a long lane. Dogs of all sizes and colors were romping around her. As I went up to her gate, I saw it was my friend Crystal. Her first words were, "Are you looking for Carey?" And then, "Yes, he is here. I saw him walking up the road and let him in the gate."

We talked a moment and I left after agreeing to come back later to pick up Carey. As I turned to go, a little black-and-white dog ran out the gate and Crystal picked her up and called her "Penny".

I woke up feeling so relieved that I had found not only my dog but my dear friend. I was never depressed about either of them again, although I still miss them both.

I related my dream to Crystal's daughter and she remarked about the little dog, "Oh! That was Pepper. She always ran in and out under foot and we had her thirteen years."

I was puzzled about the difference in her name, until one day I was talking with Crystal's daughter and cousin. The cousin remarked about a little dog Crystal's family had that was called "Penny".

The daughter remembered her as "Pepper". Both agreed it was long ago and they could not be sure is she was called "Penny" or "Pepper".

I'm convinced this was Crystal's way of helping me accept the death of my dog. She comforted me many times in life and it seems very natural to me that she could do so after death.

~E. Ruth H., Oklahoma

COLLIES

In regards to animal ghosts, I have always been able to feel their presence for a few months after their death, and during a dream almost feel their warm breath, or the shaking sound of their choke collar.

I had a Collie who was hit by a car six months after my husband died. The dog died on my husband's birthday. I felt lost and in desperation adopted a three-year old female Collie. I would sometimes dream of the dead and new collie playing together.

The female lived with us about ten years and died in our house. She just did not respond to treatment or drugs, and we checked her frequently during the night. Around 3:00am, I started to dream about my first Collie. He was running, and almost ran through me, as a ghost. I had not dreamed about him in a long time.

We woke to hear a strange dog howling in our backyard. We never saw the dog, only heard it very close, but I could immediately sense that the Collie who was ill in my family room had just died. She had, but I could also feel that she was free, very free and happy.

I have dreamed about them within a few months of her death two years ago, but never recently.

I also did dream about the first dead Collie, and other deceased relatives, when undergoing a Caesarean Section seven years ago, as I was floating under anesthesia...but it was a very comfortable, warm feeling. I did almost feel their presence, very protective.

I do believe in afterlife for pets. They are special and deserve to be eternally happy.

~ Doris S., Massachusetts

RICKEY & COOKIE

I did not see or communicate on a ghostly level but on a pre-arranged dream level. I was quite upset with having put my pet to sleep and fretted that I may have been hasty in my judgment. I asked the vet. Cookie had a chronic heart problem and could have succumbed at any time. She became progressively worse and had difficulty breathing if she was active at all. I dreaded the possibility of finding her dead. I felt so bad that I asked for a dream, a sign – anything that would let me know if I did the right thing for her.

To preface this a bit, I also had to put our previous pet, Rickey, to sleep because of age and irreversible problems – so this then is my dream.

I was in bed. Our pets have always had the run of our home and beds. Rickey jumped onto the bed beside me – a young, healthy, brightly colored red and white dog. I reacted with surprise, "Rickey, you beautiful thing!" Then in thought, "I wonder where Cookie is?" The most peaceful thought followed as if in answer. *She's running free!* Mentally, I visualized her able to run freely without breathing difficulties, examining everything as she ran. Happy!

This may have only been a dream, but I received it when asked for and it left me fully relieved. It was an experience akin to a blessing. I never asked about Rickey but she came as my messenger.

~Betsy W., Michigan

POPPI

I've had many experiences with my dead puppy. He was a beautiful Cocker Spaniel. He was an unusual dog, almost human. He understood what you said to him and to each other. He was in his seventeenth year when he died on a Friday at 10:25pm. I had him in my arms.

Seven days after he was buried, the strangest things began to happen. I have had psychic experiences before this, but I had always been told a dog had no soul. You can imagine how shocked I was. Poppi was buried in my back yard. He is in a tomb just like you would put a child in.

I was out there with my five poodles. Poppi barked the way he did when I would go out of the room. He had had a light stroke and couldn't get up by himself. I would hear Poppi walking in the hall at night, feel him jump on the bed, feel him touch me. I would even smell his decaying body. I sat in the kitchen and all at once I felt him jump in my lap. I heard all these strange noises.

For about two weeks I didn't hear anything, and then one night I was asleep and it was like someone said, "Come on." I saw myself in a huge white light. I got up and went outside. I saw Poppi coming toward me. He looked just like before he died. I started to run to him but there was a Doberman Pinscher about three feet from him. The Doberman looked like he was ready to charge if I took another step. I stopped, the big dog sat down and his body began to disappear, except for his head. Then Poppi came to me. The head disappeared. I knelt down and took Poppi in my arms.

He whined and carried on like he always did when he was glad to see me. I even felt his hair, which was coarse compared to that of my poodles. Then Poppi started to walk away.

I smiled and said, "He walks like he did when he was younger." That's the last time I heard or saw anything of Poppie. That was the first of February. He had been with me from July to February.

~Hattie H., South Carolina

SARGE

My father acquired a Newfoundland during the time he was in the military. Sarge lived with my father, grandparents, and uncle, and then later with my father and his new bride. One winter day, the dog died of what I have come to believe was bloat.

This is the same house in which I was later born. My first ever memory is as a toddler waking in my crib to see a large black dog standing protectively over me. I was frightened and cried for my mother. From later pictures labeled "Sarge," I recognized this as the dog that came to me. A Newfoundland's outline and body shape are unmistakable.

My brother later slept in that same crib in the same room with me. One afternoon I saw a large black dog walking across the room. I don't remember my brother's reaction. We didn't know it was just our dad's former dog, coming in to check on us children just that once to see if we were okay.

~Carol W., Illinois

Pictures

&

Imagery

PICTURES & IMAGERY

Many books exist on the subject of ghosts and spirits which contain pictures of human and pet spirits. Professional ghost hunters use advanced photography equipment and thermal imagery to capture spiritual pictures. Many pictures I have seen are clear images and others are only a partial view of the head or back end of a pet spirit. A few contain only white flash images on the shoulder of a person, while others have been of floating illuminated orbs.

There are spirit pictures of people and pets in the same photograph. Some of the pictures I received from pet contributors had unusual streaks of light, but I could not always make out what these images were.

Obviously these photographs held significant meaning to the pet owner, and they did not appear to me to include any type of trick photography.

I am trying to debunk the myth that all spirits are unfriendly or appear with intent to bring harm. Maybe pets reappear in spiritual imagery to simply say goodbye or to comfort the grieving owner. In some cases, it provides closure.

SONY & MAXWELL

I have pictures of my dog Maxwell, a Welsh Corgi, taken when he was a puppy. My other dog Sony (Sonja Henie) had died six months prior to my adopting Max, after a nice long life of sixteen years. She was a beautiful, white, long-haired mixed-breed.

I always joked that the pictures showed Sony's ghost directly blocking out Maxwell's face on each one, but I really assumed it was a flaw of the film.

Later I decided to show the pictures to a friend of mine who is an amateur photographer. She looked carefully and asked to see the negatives. She had no explanation and pointed out that the pictures were not sequential. Two other photos were taken in between and were clear shots of Max with a child who was visiting us.

The "ghost" did not appear until we were alone again.

~Doris K., Illionis

Unusual Pet Death

SHAKESPEARE

I'm a clairvoyant, teacher, lecturer, and writer. I teach classes in Psychic Development and through my classes, I have found many of my students hope to communicate with their pets. After they have graduated, I have found a large percentage of them do see their pets and mentally speak to them.

I, too, had a beloved pet, a beautiful white Persian named Shakespeare. At exactly 2:30pm, he was killed by a careless driver. The electricity totally shut off in the entire house and the fall of my darling cat flashed before me.

A week after his death, my husband and I were admiring the full moon in the backyard when out of the bushes came this beautiful apparition strolling past.

Shakespeare visited us for over a year, and before we moved I asked him to travel onward and to incarnate again soon. At first he was reluctant to leave and then one night he was gone.

I hope to give assurance that there is more to life than just living and dying. Even for our beloved pets.

~Joanna B., New Mexico

SUZIE and SALEY

I have lived with cats all my life. I had a terribly active female, Suzie, who was the most intelligent cat I ever had. She could think like a human being. She got wished off onto me by a woman who was going blind and thought she was giving me a male kitten.

I agreed to run an ad in the weekly paper and find a home for her, but she was so intelligent and had such a personality I would never have parted with her, not even after the first hour I had her.

Suzie was the longest, narrowest cat I ever had. When she was full-grown, she would sleep under the covers with me. She insisted I lie on my right side and when I did she would put her paws completely around my neck. Then she would stretch her hind legs straight down and dig her toenails into my legs below the knee. I am five-foot, ten inches tall, so that is one long cat!

Suzie never stayed home much once she grew up and got pregnant. I later had her spayed. She was frequently gone four days, but I would see her around the neighborhood. Usually she was with families who had a lot of cats. She would sit on the sidewalk or fence alongside the other cats.

I had another kitten, Saley, who came to me when she was about four months old. She had been abandoned, but I managed to keep her alive.

Suzie kept staying away longer and visiting my house less. After about six days, she wanted to sleep with me, and did, but she had a terrible smell about her mouth.

The next morning I took her to my regular veterinarian. Suzie had received a terrible blow on her lower jaw and had an acute bone infection which gave off the smell.

The vet gave her an anesthetic, removed all her lower teeth, and scraped the bone clean. He later admitted he had given her an overdose when she did not come out of it for longer than usual. About two days later though, she seemed to come out of it and he thought she would make a full recovery.

According to the vet, she was up and about in her cage and wanted to get out. I called that day and he told me he would like to keep her another day or so.

I had a two-story house at the time and used a large room on the lower floor as both an office and my sleeping room. I used a couch where Saley was half asleep, crouched down with her feet folded in front of her and eyes closed.

There was a table which I used as a desk, and six-foot bookshelves where Suzie enjoyed to sit and look down at me. Many times in the past she would jump down on my shoulders, hitting me with front feet on one side and hind feet on the other, and dig her claws into me to hold on. I soon learned to wear a coat when I saw her there so I wouldn't get badly clawed if she jumped down onto my shoulders.

While Suzie was recovering that final day at the vet, I sat at that table working. I felt the pressure of Suzie jumping on my shoulders as she had frequently done in the past. I reached up but could feel nothing.

The air pressure in the room rose immediately when I felt the tremendous weight of Suzie on my shoulders. The door to the hall was closed. Exactly at the time I felt this pressure, Saley stood up and stared at my shoulders. Every hair on her head, body, and tail stood straight up and her eyes were wide open! She stared at something I could not see. The weight slowly went away.

The next morning I phoned the vet and he told me the bad news. My cat had died. I said, "Yes, I know. Tell me exactly when she died."

He told me he had been there when it happened, and the time he gave me was just six or seven minutes before I felt Suzie jump on my shoulders.

~Ken K., California

DEAD MAN WITH CAT PROBLEMS

Approximately three years ago, a dear close friend of mine was brutally murdered. Since this violent deed is still unsolved, and the culprit is still amongst our society, I cannot even hint as to my identity nor where this occurred.

The deceased person had been a cat fancier, and had obtained a feline from us. After this person's demise, the feline was returned to us, which we welcomed to our home.

After several months, she had a litter of kittens, and this was a most frightening experience. We had kept a record of this feline's gestation period, as we own the stud. The day arrived for her to birth the kittens, and a cage was prepared in advance in one of our unoccupied bedrooms, so she and I could be alone and undisturbed.

As she was a bit shy in personality, about five o'clock that evening when I noticed she was getting ready to have her family, I carefully picked her up and carried her into the bedroom and closed the door.

I placed her into the prepared cage and locked it. I opened my plastic bag containing clean towels and sterilized scissors to assist if needed. She gave birth to two kittens, but couldn't do it alone. I had to spread a clean bath towel across the dresser for my work area. Each time I locked the cage after I removed a kitten or replaced it.

I suddenly felt a cold draft around my shoulders and on my legs. I wondered where the draft was coming from since the door and the window were closed. As I was staring into the cage, awaiting the next kitten, the phone rang in my kitchen. I went to answer it and carefully closed the door behind me.

I returned to the bedroom one minute later, quickly looked at the cat in the locked cage, when suddenly I was compelled to look over on the dresser. A cold freezing feeling was within my body as there on the towel on the dresser lay a dead kitten, completely clean.

How did it get there? Why was the room suddenly ice cold? The cat was unable to have more kittens. We rushed her to the vet for a C-section. We had to go to the emergency clinic since it was late at night. She had two more dead kittens. The cat had to be spayed and the first two kittens that were born normal died.

Did this happen because the deceased previous owner was unsuccessful in breeding her. Had he returned from the grave, as this was a loved favorite cat, and had a hand in all this?

How did the dead kitten get onto the dresser? And why the cold temperatures in July when it was 91 degrees outside? There were no air conditioners on, as kittens are born wet and the utmost care must be taken. Therefore, I had the window and door closed.

~Anonymous

Do Animals Have Souls

DO ANIMALS HAVE SOULS?

A regular customer recently told me a story about his late wife. She had been very sick in the hospital and the doctor urged everyone to prepare for her death. She had gone into a coma from which the doctors said she would not return.

She did wake up and the doctor said this was a miracle. He told the husband to listen carefully, because his wife would have some things to say, but it would take time after all the tubes had been removed from her throat.

Several days went by. She whispered to her husband that she was ready to die, but had been sent back from the other side to tell him that others were waiting for him in heaven.

A guide had taken her to an open field with a bridge across a stream. On the other side were all of the previous dogs her husband had owned, along with his mother and grandmother. The mother knew her son's wife and waved. She even mentioned the name of the son's first dog when he was a little boy. The husband had never told his wife that information before. The guide told the wife she could not cross the bridge at this time, but was being sent back to tell her husband she would wait for him on the other side.

God created all living things on this earth. Most religions agree man and animals are of divine origin. Some believe the body cannot be separated from the soul. Is the soul the same as the spirit? Will the spirit of man and the spirit of animals ascend to the heavens? Maybe it is the resurrection of man and the resurrection of the spirit from god that makes its way to heaven.

KEES & HEIN

An incident which happened on Election Day in 1968 has remained with me all these years, although I have never told even my family about it. We had two cats at that time, Kees and Hein.

Kees was twelve years old and had become ill with what the vet told me was a kidney problem. In the late afternoon, I glanced down the shadowy hall of our ranch home leading to the bedroom area. I glimpsed what I would have sworn was the striped and white shape of Kees running across the hall into our son's room where he always liked to sleep.

About six o'clock, the vet's office called to say Kees had died that afternoon. I have always felt in my mind that the "appearance" of Kees occurred at the moment he went.

He was only an ordinary short-haired domestic whom we had rescued from the SPCA when he was about six weeks old, but he had been our beloved family pet since then.

~ Anne L., Pennsylvania

KILLER KATIE

I grew up in a family where animals were extremely important to us. The first dog I ever remember was a Miniature Dachshund named Killer Katie. She was born six months before me. We pretty much grew up together. My mother loved Katie, who was the runt. I think that's the reason mom chose her. She was very small, even for a miniature.

Katie lived to be almost twenty. I had been taking care of the animals while my parents were out of town. I let Katie out for a minute, and when I came back she had fallen into the goldfish pond and drowned. My mother wasn't mad at me. Surprisingly enough, she said Katie had a good long life that most dogs never got.

Katie was so protective of my mother. She would never leave her side. To this day I don't think she has. Our home is a two-story with hardwood floors throughout the downstairs.

Katie's little legs were so small she had to be carried up the steps. When we would go upstairs at night to watch television, Katie would pace around the staircase until one of us would run down there and carry her up. Some nights we can still hear her little nails on the wood floor as she paces around waiting for mom to come get her.

Although she lived a long life, she wasn't ready to leave.

After Katie's death, a friend and I were playing Ouija board at my house. We asked my mom if she had any questions. Of course her only questions were where her animals were.

The board responded quickly, "Waiting for you."

We already knew this, but it still took us by surprise. I believe few people share the kind of love me and my family do for animals. I don't think I'll ever completely get over any of my animals' deaths. My only comfort is that I know I will at some point be reunited with them.

~Jennifer M., Texas

20-YEAR OLD DOG

As almighty God created heaven and earth and all creatures great and small, surely he has prepared a heavenly afterlife for them as well. Our pets know more about loyalty, devotion and forgiveness than we do. They comfort us with their love, whether we are rich or poor. Surely these pets who have so enriched our lives are now spirits to exist forever and ever. I feel they can be our guardian angels.

Shortly after my dog died at age twenty, she came to me clearly in a dream – running amid brilliant green grass with a happy expression on her face indicating she was now whole again to run and play. We were so close to each other; I'm sure she wanted me to know she was free of the confines of old age and would be in that special place waiting for me.

~Eleanor V., Pennsylvania

GWENDOLYN

Gwen was a lively Lhasa Apso, pure white with a slightly curly coat. She knew what she wanted and would convey her wishes in no uncertain terms. I named her Gwendolyn St. Nicholas as she was "white-browed" and born on December 6th.

When she became seriously ill at Thanksgiving, after being my companion for twelve years, I was grief stricken. Gwen was diagnosed with a liver disease and given a prognosis of six months at best. We had only six precious weeks.

The last weeks of Gwen's life were regimented by special diets, coaxing her to eat, and struggles to take medications. At the end, she suffered a stroke. When I finally accepted death was inevitable, I chose euthanasia.

That night after her death I was inconsolable. I knelt at my bedside and cried out to God to send me a vision so I would know Gwen's spirit lived on and that she was not alone. Instantly Christ was at my left side. I could see the hem of His robe and His sandaled feet. He assured me Gwen lived on and the things of earth that demonstrated God's pure love would not be lost to us. They would be in heaven waiting for us.

Then I saw a vision of us walking up steps to a mansion of marble and gold. Upon entering, I noticed a large room where I could see small pets at a distance. We started to climb a staircase where I discovered a niche holding a gilded birdcage. In the cage was a finch named Mike, a pet from my childhood. As we climbed further, I noticed a window where I could see another mansion. I recognized two cats and a dog who had belonged to my parents.

At the top of the stairs was a room to the right. There I found a golden bed covered in white satin and lace. On the bed were two pillows, one at the head and one along the near side of the bed. I *knew* they were for two Chihuahuas I had through childhood and young adulthood. In front of the footboard was a golden bed shaped like a crown. It had multi-hued stones encrusted in its top. Jesus then told me this was a bed for Gwen.

I asked Him why this bed was for her and not the others. He gently replied that Gwen had earned it. This was her reward, for Gwen had been with me through the most difficult and challenging years of my life: through job changes, moves, breakups, loss of friends, home and financial insecurities, and devastating surgery. Through all those hard times Gwen had been the one constant in my life. She gave me so much love during her lifetime and unconditionally accepted mine in return. She offered me the opportunity to learn many lessons during her life, and even more love and opportunities in her death.

I believe in this vision. I lack the imagination to have "dreamed" this vision. It has helped me in the grieving days following her death.

Best of all, it has reassured me my Gwenny-Girl lives on. Someday we shall be reunited.

~Nancy G., Indiana

PATTY & PAMWAM

I once owned two darling black and white Chihuahuas. They were very intelligent little things and I gave them the run of my big home.

I didn't know they hadn't had their shots; I took for granted that they had. One cold fall day little Patty was suddenly taken deathly sick. I rushed her to the vet. She had distemper. Pamwam became ill with it, too, and finally died. Patty lived, but she was subjected to seizures every now and then, especially when she ate something rich.

My gardener Bob lived next to me in a trailer. One day he saw little Patty having a seizure. He talked me into having her put to sleep. I will admit that for some time I had contemplated having Patty put to sleep, and often wondered if dogs really did survive death. I was almost sure they did.

So one day I drove into town with Patty, and the vet gave her the needle and put her to sleep. When I brought her little body home, Bob took it and tenderly buried it out by the lilac bush with all the other dogs looking on. I asked God to please give me some revelation that Patty and other dogs lived on.

I had seven other dogs, Prissy being the mother of all the rest. They were particularly fond of me and always insisted I put them to bed every night.

That night after Patty was buried and the other dogs were put to bed, they were very, very restless. This was unusual, for they were all sound sleepers. Prissy, the mother, kept coming into my bedroom; then she would go through the whole house. And then the other ones would get up and walk the floors. It was a restless and fitful night.

The next morning Bob came into the kitchen and said, "Well, I dreamed last night that Patty came back and brought bones for all the other dogs."

I am positive (almost) that little Patty came back and haunted the place and contacted them, and the house in general. Anyway, she must have been trying to make herself known to the other dogs, and to me also.

~Ruth B., California

Pet

Interventions

To Save Humans

PET INTERVENTIONS TO SAVE HUMANS

This section of the book contains incidences where a pet has returned to save the owner from dangerous situations. It is possible that their presence is always with us, but just not in the living.

Some pets have returned from the other-side years later to wake their owner when a fire has broken out while they were sound asleep. The spirits of passed pets have returned to scratch on the door to distract their human companion from a heavy chest which would have fallen on them (as noted in this chapter). Others have returned to warn them of a washed-out road ahead where they would have driven off a cliff.

I have read several books which discuss intriguing life-and-death situations focusing on a pet's return from the other-side to save their owner from impending doom. Some individuals will never believe these stories and cannot be convinced until it happens to them. These reappearances from deceased pets suggest an everlasting bond that even death cannot destroy.

ANIMALS HAVE PSYCHIC POWERS

Reprinted from *The National Enquirer* (November 8, 1977)

A Colorado motorist stopped his car on a mountain road late at night when his headlights picked out his Collie, which had died a year earlier.

The motorist found the road had been washed away and his car would have plunged over a cliff if he had continued.

SOME STEPS BEYOND

In 1940 a reverend and his wife were living in California. She was superintendent of a convalescent hospital at the time. In late winter she was summoned to the hospital in the middle of the night because a patient was dying. She got into her uniform and set out. The adjoining block was lonely with no houses or street lights. As she left the lighted area a small car with two men in it careened around the corner and pulled up beside her. She started to run but the car followed slowly.

All of a sudden their big white Collie raced up and planted himself between her and the car. She saw one of the men lean out and look at him before the two took off in a hurry. The dog stayed with her until she reached the next street light. Then he was gone.

And only then, recovering from her fright, did she realize that the protective Collie had died several months before. She wrote, "My husband is a minister of a well-known Protestant church. We are not superstitious or overly imaginative — but we know that sometimes God moves in mysterious ways."

~Anonymous

TRIXIE

When I was a teenager, we had a Fox Terrier named Trixie. One day mom was pulling hard to open a stuck drawer in a chest. On top of the chest was a trunk, and on top of the trunk was an upright footlocker. As mom pulled at the drawer, she heard Trixie scratching urgently at the side door. Mom stepped over to open the door, and the footlocker fell from the stack and landed where mom had been standing.

Mom always said Trixie saved her life that day.

Please understand... Trixie had died a short time before this incident happened.

~Ruth R., Florida

In

Conclusion

IN CONCLUSION

Man has always tried to make some sense of order in the world. We separate ourselves by religion, by country and by language. We align ourselves by the stars and set up calendars to bring predictability to our lives. We remember birthdays and anniversaries to commemorate things from the past and celebrate religious events. We use time to record things in history and we try to interpret daily life. We use science to enhance and improve our lives.

Your own spirit and soul already feel a connection to the rest of the universe and depending on your faith, a connection to the heavens. You may not be able to touch it but you believe and sense its reality.

Based on the personal accounts gathered, pet owners around the country felt a spiritual connection between themselves and their beloved pet that passed away. The stories they contributed to this volume cannot be scientifically explained yet the writers know in their heart what spiritual happening occurred.

I grew up left-handed. My perspective has always been different and more abstract than the right-handers of this world. Teachers always tried to take the odd-shaped peg and shove it through the square-shaped hole. Most tried to get me to conform to their perspective of the world and that was not good enough for me.

A friend of mine would get whacked by nuns if he tried to write left-handed. The nuns made him wear a sling to force him to write like a right-hander. He developed a terrible speech impediment from his fear of the nuns. Lefties were considered unnatural and evil.

I've tried to take these personal stories and make some sense of the world. I looked to find common happenings that could be categorized. Did another person have any experience similar to someone else?

My left-handed abstractness tried to categorize these stories. Just read with an open mind. After receiving and reading over 100 stories from pet owners around the country, I charted the similarities.

I tried to break them down: pet spirit that lingers, sensation of the pet's death, other pets recognizing the departed pet, physical objects being disturbed, semi-sleep experiences, daytime experiences, the sense of touch, the sense of hearing, the sense of sight, distinct characteristics of the former pet, telepathy, dreams and reality. These stories were written by the pet owner in their hand and from their heart. When I requested stories from pet owners in magazines they knew they were not alone in these spiritual happenings. I believe many were searching for answers as to whether they would be reunited in heaven with their pet.

By now I hope you've read all the stories sent by pet owners about their beloved pet and the experiences they had after their passing. Some saw the spirit of their deceased pet and also of a passed relative. Many objects were moved and others experienced audio sounds and certain aromas associated with a passed pet. Pets sometimes reacted as if seeing something humans did not, hissing and clawing at the invisible. Of course some pet owners are better writers than others but all of the stories come directly from the heart.

I do believe these stories suggest a pet's spirit or soul exists even after death, just as with people. There is no doubt in my mind that one day I will be reunited with all of my cherished pets in heaven. I have experienced many spiritual happenings that correlate to my opinions on animal after-life.

The day after my beloved German Shepherd, Prancer, passed away, I was greeted by a single, large hawk feather lying at the back door of my pet store. According to my faith, the feather signifies a spiritual rebirth. I interpreted this as a sign of Prancer's acceptance into the gates of heaven.

I heard the spirit of my pet guinea pig for months after its passing. The spirit of my pet cat roamed the outside of my house for months after his passing as well.

We can debate all day long from scriptures that pets might or might not ascend to heaven. I'm not a theologian but have interviewed many religious experts that have given opinions for and against pets going to heaven.

I can only go by what my heart says and what my faith tells me. Based on your own religious belief, you may determine if the cherished pets of the world go to heaven. The memory and spirit of our beloved pets, however, will be forever imprinted in our minds and our hearts.

AMEN / APETS

PHOTO ACKNOWLEDGEMENTS

Used under Creative Commons licensing.

Sun Through Trees and Fog: fotocommunity.com/pc/pc/display/10358827
F.W. Murphy: en.wikipedia.org/wiki/File:Cat_November_2010-1a.jpg
Kirby's Ghost: flickr.com/photos/27117620@N06/5992470306/
Dusty: commons.wikimedia.org/wiki/File:So_happy_smiling_cat.jpg
German Shepherd Plus One: pixabay.com/en/dog-german-shepherd-garden-grass-115892/
Babe: pixabay.com/en/shetland-sheepdog-dog-sheltie-cute-165014/
Big Dog: flickr.com/photos/kylemay/1455925735/
Leaky: en.wikipedia.org/wiki/Purebred_dog
Goliath: flickr.com/photos/theodorescott/3384066882/
Blossom: en.wikipedia.org/wiki/Rage_syndrome
Gigi: en.wikipedia.org/wiki/Bolognese_dog
Honey & Gypsy: commons.wikimedia.org/wiki/File:Seal_Old_Style_Siamese_Thai.jpg
Bunnie: flickr.com/photos/lindseywb/3526128123/
Lucky: commons.wikimedia.org/wiki/File:Australian_Shepherd_rot_tricolor.jpg
Pepe & Kemo: commons.wikimedia.org/wiki/File:Pastor_alem%C3%A1n_galego.JPG
Leo: commons.wikimedia.org/wiki/File:Feral_cat_Virginia_crop.jpg
Sock: commons.wikimedia.org/wiki/File:Ranger_Jeff's_Quarter_Horse_Peter.jpg
Snowball: pixabay.com/en/cat-kitten-black-wet-sour-4465/
Penny: flickr.com/photos/fakeplasticalice/3140660338/
Snowball II: commons.wikimedia.org/wiki/File:Szusza_pekingese.jpg
Eeaoo: flickr.com/photos/meaganjean/5581243984/
Laird: pixabay.com/en/border-collie-herding-dog-canine-191776/
Kat: flickr.com/photos/brownpau/4154922277/
Dushus: commons.wikimedia.org/wiki/File:Pal_as_Lassie_1942.JPG
Smokey: commons.wikimedia.org/wiki/File:Cody_the_Cockapoo.jpg
Pinched Nose: commons.wikimedia.org/wiki/File:Dog's_Love.jpg
Critter: flickr.com/photos/chiropractic/3105754589/
Taffy: commons.wikimedia.org/wiki/File:Pet_dog_fetching_sticks_in_Wales-3April2010.jpg
Canary: flickr.com/photos/majd192/5341039692/
Schnauzer: flickr.com/photos/greggoconnell/386728530/
Zak: cats.about.com/u/sty/blackcats/whyiloveblackcats/Spooky.1S60.htm
Katy: commons.wikimedia.org/wiki/File:Cute_grey_kitten.jpg
Missy: flickr.com/photos/arice/750801539/
Curtis: en.wikipedia.org/wiki/Boxer_(dog)
Out to Pasture: commons.wikimedia.org/wiki/File:Doberman_Pinscher_red_standing.jpg
Fluffy: flickr.com/photos/monsieurgordon/3839985251/
Mitty: flickr.com/photos/trickypink/2760577210/
Dax: flickr.com/photos/gorgeouspot/2352080540
Trixie & Zippy: commons.wikimedia.org/wiki/File:Rat_terrier_sleeping.jpg
Tippy: flickr.com/photos/fuzzy/6293711476/
Caramel: flickr.com/photos/94801434@N00/3845053837
Freckles & The Ghost: flickr.com/photos/15049511@N00/752540021
Magick?: flickr.com/photos/60003305@N00/280809080

Bandit: flickr.com/photos/kmonojo/384544629/in
Simon: flickr.com/photos/steevithak/767028469
Sheila: flickr.com/photos/epicsurfgt/209817009
Judy: flickr.com/photos/aegidian/6854866350/
Missy: flickr.com/photos/chitrasudar/26545641
Tiny: flickr.com/photos/sloan_g/2929965846/
Tomasina: flickr.com/photos/gattou/2232923171
Vera: en.wikipedia.org/wiki/Savannah_monitor
Gemini: flickr.com/photos/ashleybayles/5949583068
Flash: flickr.com/photos/mindfrieze/8183763968
Boxer & Siamese Experience: flickr.com/photos/wiki/39606141;
flickr.com/photos/gsloan/3631165494
Bobbi: commons.wikimedia.org/wiki/File:Sadie_005.jpg
Sprite: flickr.com/photos/27117620@N06/10505159513
Gemeni: commons.wikimedia.org/wiki/File:Young_Siamese_Seal_Point.jpg
Princess: flickr.com/photos/ampm/3481540472
Bentley: flickr.com/photos/tigergirl/4065433212
Crybaby: flickr.com/photos/titkov/8643704072
Patches: flickr.com/photos/beauvais/3736228737
Heidi: flickr.com/photos/westmidlandspolice/6754609761
Bunjie: flickr.com/photos/osuduff/434219012
The Cocker: flickr.com/photos/maxiharmony/8270280828/
Shadow Cat: commons.wikimedia.org/wiki/File%3AShadow_cat.jpg
Sam: flickr.com/photos/leeco/30784736
Psychic Chihuahua: flickr.com/photos/dancentury/5652300564
Ghost Cat: flickr.com/photos/36979785@N06/5711805613
Rocky: flickr.com/photos/macsurak/13085285604
Carey: en.wikipedia.org/wiki/Belgian_Shepherd
Collies: en.wikipedia.org/wiki/Border_Collie
Rickey & Cookie: commons.wikimedia.org/wiki/File:Orange_%26_White_American_Brittany.jpg
Poppi: commons.wikimedia.org/wiki/File:Bo_the_poodle_retrieving_a_duck.jpg
Sarge: commons.wikimedia.org/wiki/File:Newfoundland_dog_001.jpg
Sony & Maxwell: commons.wikimedia.org/wiki/File:Mixed-breed_dog_white_sleeping.jpg
Shakespeare: commons.wikimedia.org/wiki/File:PersanBlanc.jpg
Suzie & Saley: commons.wikimedia.org/wiki/File:Longcat_(6435769739).jpg
Dead Man with Cat Problems: flickr.com/photos/jsome1/3239689523
Kees & Hain: commons.wikimedia.org/wiki/File:Tabby-cat-domestic-shorthair-force.jpg
Killer Katie: commons.wikimedia.org/wiki/File:Smooth_Miniature_Dachshund_puppy.jpg
20 year old dog: pixabay.com/en/dog-alone-green-grass-lawn-spring-338431/
Gwendolyn: commons.wikimedia.org/wiki/File:Lhasa_apso_%22yuna%22.JPG
Patty & Pamwam: flickr.com/photos/dmuth/5910237359/
Trixie: pixabay.com/en/fox-terrier-smooth-fox-terrier-164373/